"The rise of anxiety and depression among teens today is alarmi  ded more than ever. In this workbook, Michael Tompkins offers acces can immediately put into action to feel better and strengthen their ag be among my newest go-tos in my own work as a child psychologist, of two teens."

—**Anatasia S. Kim, PhD**, professor of clinical psychology at The Wright Institute, and coauthor of *It's Time to Talk (and Listen)* and *Clinical Psychology Internship for Underrepresented Students*

"A comprehensive, clever, and engaging workbook stocked with all the key cognitive behavioral therapy (CBT) interventions yet adapted for the realities of modern adolescence. In *The Anxiety and Depression Workbook for Teens*, Tompkins respectfully guides teens in how to target their anxiety and mood through the application of thirty-seven relevant ideas, including handling life's hard knocks, recovering from mistakes, time management, coping with homework demands, and conflict resolution. Teens everywhere will benefit from this treasure trove of wisdom."

—**Katherine Martinez, PsyD, RPsych**, director of www.behaviouralparenting.com, consultant for Anxiety Canada, and coauthor of *Getting Comfortable with Uncertainty for Teens*

"I like a book that gets right to solutions to two of the most common problems teens face—anxiety and depression. Michael Tompkins does just that. This book is full of straightforward, actionable, and effective ways to defeat these problems. I highly recommend this excellent workbook for all families of adolescents, as the tools in this book will decrease common suffering and increase success."

—**Jennifer Shannon, LMFT**, author of *The Shyness and Social Anxiety Workbook for Teens*

"Tompkins makes another masterful, impressive contribution to teenage mental wellness. With compassion, he coaches teens in specific CBT steps to tackle anxiety, worry, and depression triggered by the challenges of adolescence. This warmly relatable workbook is immediately useful with downloadable exercises. Embracing his outlined steps moves readers toward a valued life with friends, family, school, and beyond. I highly recommend this transformative resource to teens, parents, teachers, and counselors."

—**Elaine Elliott-Moskwa, PhD**, president of the Academy of Cognitive and Behavioral Therapies, and author of *The Growth Mindset Workbook*

"I love the science-based, bite-sized lessons in this new workbook by Michael Tompkins! Each one offers a simple technique for boosting mood and quieting anxiety. I'm grateful to Michael that I'll be able to point teens, parents, and therapists toward this excellent resource. It will be invaluable for countless teens who are struggling to find their way through anxiety or depression."

—**Seth J. Gillihan, PhD**, author of *Mindful Cognitive Behavioral Therapy*, and coauthor of *CBT Deck for Kids and Teens*

"Michael Tompkins has once again stepped up to answer the call to offer encouragement, compassion, and research-based strategies to support teens. *The Anxiety and Depression Workbook for Teens* skillfully provides both strategies and knowledge to bring agency and hope to address the number one mental health concern facing teens. This thoughtful workbook is for teens, but people of all ages would benefit as well."

—**Rona Renner, RN**, author of *Is That Me Yelling?*

"Making science-informed psychosocial interventions accessible to lay audiences is challenging. With *The Anxiety and Depression Workbook for Teens*, master clinician Michael Tompkins meets this challenge head-on with another excellent self-help guide that is readable, practical, and filled with valuable exercises. The techniques contained in this exceptional tool kit are firmly rooted in empirical data supporting treatments that work. Finally, Tompkins's skillfulness in bringing these effective procedures to life is highly laudable."

—**Robert D. Friedberg, PhD, ABPP**, professor, head of pediatric behavioral health emphasis area, and director of the Center for the Study and Treatment of Anxious Youth at Palo Alto University

"If you are a teenager who deals with anxiety or depression, this book is for you! Each chapter gives you scientifically proven strategies to tackle the unique problems that come with anxiety and depression. Tompkins's writing is easy to follow, and you will relate to the stories he shares about other teens. You don't even need to read the entire book. You can zero in on exactly what you need to help yourself right away."

—**Bridget Flynn Walker, PhD**, clinical psychologist specializing in the assessment and treatment of individuals with anxiety and related disorders, and author of *Anxiety Relief for Kids* and *Social Anxiety Relief for Teens*

"Michael Tompkins offers an excellent array of activities to help teens effectively manage their anxiety and depression. The skills are described in clear, uncomplicated terms, and, importantly, they are presented in a way that facilitates participation in them quickly. I highly recommend *The Anxiety and Depression Workbook for Teens* to any teen who is struggling to cope with anxiety or depression."

—**R. Trent Codd, III, EdS**, vice president of clinical services for the Carolinas, Refresh Mental Health; and coauthor of *Socratic Questioning for Therapists and Counselors*

the anxiety & depression workbook for teens

simple cbt skills to help you deal with anxiety, worry & sadness

MICHAEL A. TOMPKINS, PhD

Instant Help Books
An Imprint of New Harbinger Publications, Inc.

Publisher's Note

This publication is designed to provide accurate and authoritative information in regard to the subject matter covered. It is sold with the understanding that the publisher is not engaged in rendering psychological, financial, legal, or other professional services. If expert assistance or counseling is needed, the services of a competent professional should be sought.

INSTANT HELP, the Clock Logo, and NEW HARBINGER are trademarks of New Harbinger Publications, Inc.

New Harbinger Publications is an employee-owned company.

Instant Help Books
An imprint of New Harbinger Publications, Inc.
5720 Shattuck Avenue
Oakland, CA 94609
www.newharbinger.com

Cover design by Amy Shoup

Acquired by Tesilya Hanauer

Edited by Jean Blomquist

Library of Congress Cataloging-in-Publication Data on file

Printed in the United States of America

27 26 25

10 9 8 7 6 5 4 3

For Mady and Livie

Amazing teens once, amazing women now.

contents

note to professionals

The skills in this workbook are taken from cognitive behavioral therapy, a practical and evidence-based approach to the treatment of anxiety and mood disorders in adults and teenagers. Although there are many cognitive behavioral skills that can help anxious or depressed teens, this workbook includes those activities that I believe can facilitate your important work with your teen clients. You can select particular activities to include in a counseling session or send activities home with teens as therapeutic homework. At times, teens will have trouble practicing activities because they believe that they're too anxious or depressed to do them. This is an opportunity for teens to learn, with your support, that they can do more than they believe they can in the moment, regardless of how anxious or depressed they feel. At other times, an activity may increase a teen's anxious or depressed mood because it invites them to think about difficult problems. At such times, teens will benefit from your emotional support and encouragement to think about and work on the problems that trouble them.

Counselors play an important role in teaching teens effective tools to manage the anxiety and sadness that can arise as they navigate our complicated and ever-changing world. These tools in your hands can make a big difference for the teens in your care. I hope this workbook supports the important and life-changing work you do. As a mental health professional, as a parent of young adults who were once teens, and as a man who was once a teen himself, I thank you.

introduction

If you purchased this workbook or someone gave it to you, you're likely feeling anxious, depressed, or both. Now, everyone has a passing case of "the blues" when a friendship hits a bump, or they feel anxious when facing exams or college applications. But maybe you've had these feelings in ways that are really intense—feelings of sadness or despair that make life hard and just don't pass, or experiences of anxiety that are extreme and make it hard for you to focus or do what you want to do. Maybe you've experienced both depression and anxiety at the same time. This isn't uncommon. In fact, people who experience bouts of depression likely experience intense feelings of anxiety too. Whether these feelings are mild or intense, or whether they're a temporary reaction to something happening in your life or they've persisted for many years, the activities in this workbook can help.

In this workbook, you'll find activities that help you understand how anxiety and depression work. For example, you'll learn to identify the thinking traps you might fall into—meaning, the biased ways you think about situations and events, which may drive the depression and anxiety you feel—and skills to resist falling into those thinking traps in the future, so anxiety and depression have less of a hold on your life. You'll also learn skills to solve problems, break tasks down to get projects moving, communicate clearly, and stand up for yourself, to name just a few. You'll notice that there are many activities in the workbook, because there are many skills that you can learn to manage your anxiety and depression. Some skills will work great for you, and other skills will not work so well. That's okay. No two people are the same, and therefore no two people are anxious or depressed in the same way and for the same reasons. That's why you'll want to try all the activities in this book, to learn which skills work the best for you.

Although these activities can help decrease your anxiety and depression, they'll only help if you practice them. No doubt you've learned this lesson many times, whether you're practicing your free-throw shot, practicing the flute, or practicing algebra calculations: regular practice makes a difference. This is particularly true for skills to manage your anxiety and depression. Of course, you also know it's always more difficult to practice a skill when you're feeling anxious and depressed. For example, it's always easier to take a shot from the free-throw line or play the flute when you're relaxed, confident, and feeling good about yourself than it is when you're feeling anxious or depressed. Therefore, it's important to practice the activities enough so that you can use them effectively and automatically no matter how anxious or down you feel.

This workbook isn't intended to replace other kinds of help, such as counseling or medications, but to add to the kinds of help you're already receiving. Many counselors use workbooks like this to help anxious or depressed people. If your anxious or depressed feelings persist after practicing the skills in the workbook for a few weeks or months, you might want to seek the support of a counselor who can help tailor the activities to fit you and your specific circumstances. In particular, if your anxiety or depression worsens over time, and if you're having thoughts of hurting yourself, tell a caring adult who can keep you safe while you find a counselor who can help.

Over time, as you learn and practice the activities in this workbook, you'll begin to feel less anxious and down and more comfortable and optimistic about your future and yourself. Over time, these skills will become second nature to you, and that's when the real change happens. Your life will grow and open as your future fills with the hope and good things that you deserve. It just takes patience, practice, and a little time.

Note: Various worksheets and other materials, including meditations, are available for download at the website for this book: http://www.newharbinger.com/49197.

1 about anxiety and depression

for you to know

Anxiety and sadness are normal human experiences. These feelings signal that there is a current or future problem that you may want to solve. Learning what anxiety and depression are and are not is the first step toward learning to manage these experiences.

From time to time, everyone feels more anxious or sad than usual. These feelings are helpful when they come and go. It's when these feelings persist and intensify over months and years that they become unhelpful. For example, depression is when normal sadness persists and intensifies. An anxiety disorder is when normal anxiety persists and intensifies. When this happens, these once helpful feelings create long-term problems for you. You might lose friends because you feel too anxious to go to parties with them, or they drop you because they're tired of your angry outbursts and doom-and-gloom attitude. You might quit school because you feel too depressed or anxious to attend.

You likely experience deep and lasting feelings of anxiety and depression for several reasons:

- **Nature**: You may know a biological relative who struggles with excessive anxiety and depression too. You inherited this tendency to have deep and lasting feelings of anxiety and depression from biological relatives. This is the genetic part of excessive anxiety and depression. In fact, what you inherited is called high emotional reactivity. *Emotional reactivity* is the tendency to have strong and persistent emotional reactions to life events. In other words, if you have high emotional reactivity, even small stressful life events can cause you to feel intensely anxious or down, and it takes longer for your emotional system to bounce back than for people with a more typical level of emotional reactivity.

- **Nurture**: People learn from life events and from other people. Most things we learn are helpful, but when you struggle with excessive anxiety and depression, you likely learned unhelpful ways to think about yourself and about life events that intensify and maintain your anxious and depressed feelings. You probably learned this way of thinking from important people in your life or from the difficulties you've experienced.
- **Interaction**: Although nature and nurture play a role in your anxious and depressed feelings, it's the interaction between these two things that influences how you respond to life events. Not all people react the same way to the same life event. That's because different people have different genetics and different people think about events in different ways.

Although you can't change your biology, you can change the way you think and act when you're feeling anxious or depressed. Learning to change how you think and respond can make the difference between whether you feel anxious or down for a few hours or for a few days, weeks, or months. That's where this workbook comes in. With this workbook, you can learn to change the way you think about and respond to life events. As you change these things, you'll feel less anxious and depressed today and tomorrow.

for you to do

As you've heard, "The apple doesn't fall too far from the tree." On the family tree below, write the names of biological family members or loved ones (grandparents, parents, aunts, uncles, siblings) who are anxious, depressed, or both. Feel free to add any branches that might be missing from the diagram. Write next to each name A for anxiety, D for depression, and AD for both anxiety and depression.

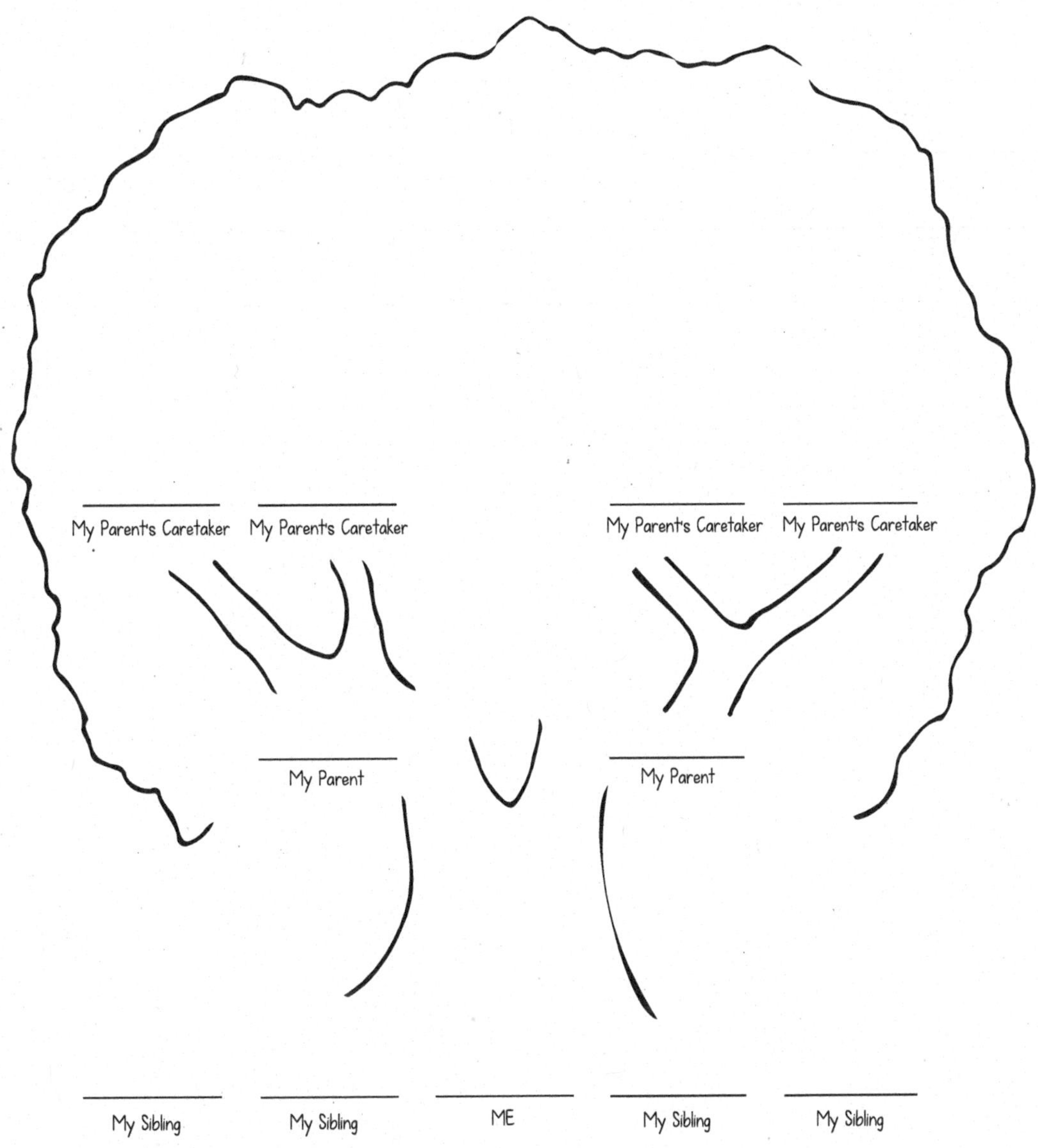

Describe what you've learned from relatives that tends to fuel your anxious and depressed feelings.

____

____

____

____

____

____

____

____

more to do

There are many signals that indicate you're feeling more than the usual levels of anxiety and depression. You may notice that some signals are common to both excessive anxiety and depression. Circle any that you've experienced or are experiencing now:

Anxiety Signals		Depression Signals	
Avoidance	Rapid heart beat	Aches and pains	Irritable
Chest pain	Restlessness	Desire to be alone	Negative attitude
Constant worry	Sweating	Feel helpless	No interest in activities
Difficulty breathing	Tired	Feel hopeless	Significant weight change
Feel on edge	Trembling	Feel like a failure	Thoughts of hurting self
Irritable	Trouble breathing	Feel worthless	Trouble concentrating
Jittery	Trouble concentrating	Forgetfulness	Trouble sleeping
Feel like you're going crazy	Trouble sleeping	Frequent crying	Unhappiness
	Upset stomach	Guilty feelings	Withdrawal from friends

Describe anxiety or depression signals that you've experienced that aren't listed.

____

____

____

2 prepare to change

for you to know

Learning and practicing skills that will help you feel less anxious and depressed can be difficult at first. Identifying and connecting with your core values, the core of who you are and what's deeply important to you, can help you change the ingrained habits that intensify and maintain your anxiety and depression.

Think back to the last scene of *The Wizard of Oz*: Dorothy and her friends—Lion, Scarecrow, and Tin Man—stand together. As they say good-bye to each other, the wizard honors their unique core values. For the Lion, it's courage. For the Scarecrow, it's intelligence. For the Tin Man, it's love, and for Dorothy, it's family. Imagine that you're standing there too. What would your core values be? Is friendship one of your core values? If yes, this might explain how much time and effort you're willing to put into making your friendships caring and supportive. Is creativity one of your core values? If yes, this might explain your passion for drawing or music. Is it achievement? If yes, this might explain your willingness to practice your free-throw shots over and over. Core values are the personal beliefs and principles that guide how you wish to live your life, what you wish to stand for, and who you wish to be. Core values are the internal compass points that guide you in the direction you wish to live your life.

for you to do

In the table below, circle the five core values, out of all the ones that are listed, that are most important to you. Feel free to add other core values to the list:

Values About Family/Friends	Values About School/Sports/Work
Being fun loving	Curiosity
Dependability	Achievement
Harmony	Knowledge
Helpfulness	Leadership
Honesty	Teamwork
Loyalty	Excellence
____________	____________
____________	____________

Values About Play/Creativity	Values About Health/Well-Being
Beauty	Self-care
Freedom	Endurance
Harmony	Self-reliance
Imagination	Balance
Innovation	Fitness
Uniqueness	Self-improvement
____________	____________
____________	____________

List the core values that you didn't know were important to you.

___

___

___

___

Are there any core values you thought were important to you and discovered that they were less important than you thought?

___

___

___

___

more to do

Now that you know the core values that are important to you, next consider how working to feel less anxious and depressed fits with those core values. For example, if you identified harmonious relationships with your family and friends as a core value, how does your anxiety or depression affect your relationships? Are you more irritable with your friends? If imagination and achievement are core values for you, how does your anxiety and depression affect your ability to do well in school or in a play or concert? Do you put off homework because you're worried that you might not do it well? If honesty and loyalty are core values for you, how do anxiety and depression affect your ability to be the kind of friend you want to be? When you're anxious about attending a party, do you tell friends you're sick? How could you start to change some of these patterns to pursue what matters to you?

Describe how connecting with your core values can help you overcome the anxiety and depression that holds you back.

___

___

___

___

___

___

___

___

___

___

3 the ABCs of anxiety and depression

for you to know

Your thoughts and actions play a role in the intensity and duration of your anxious or depressed feelings. When you understand these anxious and depressed patterns, you can better manage these feelings. Learning the ABCs of your anxious and depressed feelings can help you identify your anxious and depressed patterns.

Armin knew he was moody. He'd been this way all his life. Although he did okay in his classes, he worried about his grades. Although he had friends, he worried that other kids, even his friends, didn't like him. He could feel really down on the weekends if he wasn't busy, and he spent a lot of time alone because he was either too nervous to hang out with people or too down to get out of bed. Although Armin knew he was moody, he didn't know why.

One day, Armin decided to go to the counseling office. The counselor asked Armin if he knew what made him feel anxious or depressed. When Armin shrugged his shoulders, the counselor said, "When you learned to read, you first learned your ABCs. It's time for you to learn the ABCs of feelings." The counselor then wrote on the board:

- **A is for antecedent**: These are the events, situations, or people that tend to trigger your anxious or depressed feelings.
- **B is for belief**: These are the thoughts or pictures that run through your mind when you're feeling anxious or depressed.
- **C is for consequence**: This is what you're feeling and how intensely you feel anxious or depressed.

The counselor then gave Armin an ABC log and asked him to keep track of when he felt anxious or depressed, or both. Armin recorded and rated his anxiety and depression for a week. Part of his log is below. He realized that he tended to worry that people thought he was stupid or bad at something. He also realized that he felt the most depressed when he was alone on the weekends. As Armin learned his ABCs of anxiety and depression, he started to make some small changes, like trying to do something with his best friend on the weekends, or saying hi to kids he doesn't know well.

Day/Time	Antecedent	Belief	Consequence
Tuesday, 4 p.m.	Working on English essay that's due tomorrow.	What's the point of trying. I don't know what I'm doing. I'm just going to fail the class.	Anxious (4) Depressed (8)
Wednesday, 11:30 a.m.	Working on physics lab with Jason, Jenna, and Wilson.	They all know this stuff way better than me. They probably think I'm stupid.	Anxious (6)
Thursday, 3 p.m.	Walking home from school with Wilson. He's talking about the math test tomorrow.	He's going to ace the test. He thinks I'm stupid and that I'm going to fail the test	Anxious (5)
Friday, 8 p.m.	At a pizza party with my team after the soccer match.	Everyone's thinking that I'm the worst player on the team.	Anxious (4)
Saturday, 9:30 p.m.	In my room reading Jason's social media feed. I read about the fun stuff he's doing.	I never do anything fun. I'm such a loser.	Depressed (8)
Sunday, 1 p.m.	At soccer practice, and Wilson runs over and gives me a couple of tips on my passes.	He's a cool guy. He probably thinks I can use some tips, and he's right.	Anxious (2)

for you to do

To learn your ABCs of anxiety and depression, record your ABCs of anxiety and depression for at least a week. Make as many copies of the blank My ABC Log on the next page as you need or download several blank copies from http://www.newharbinger.com/49197.

My ABC Log

Instructions: In the **A** column, write what triggered your anxious or depressed feelings. In the **B** column, write what you were thinking when you were feeling anxious or depressed. In the **C** column, write how much anxiety or depression you were feeling (where 1 is low and 10 is high).

Day/Time	**A**ntecedent	**B**elief	**C**onsequence

more to do

When you have a week or two of ABC logs, look over them and answer these questions:

What was it like to pay attention to your anxious and depressed feelings? Did keeping the log make you more or less anxious or depressed?

___

___

___

Were there times when you felt both anxious and depressed? Why?

___

___

___

Describe any patterns you noticed over time. Did the same events or situations tend to make you anxious or depressed? Did you tend to have the same beliefs or thoughts each time you felt anxious or depressed?

___

___

___

4 identify your thinking traps

for you to know

Thinking traps are the unhelpful ways you think about events and yourself that keep you trapped in intense feelings of anxiety and depression. Thinking traps are automatic, but once you learn to identify them, you'll be able to quickly climb out of these traps to feel better.

Gabriel is playing chess with Ms. Valdez, who is Gabriel's math teacher and sponsors the chess club. It's Gabriel's turn, but he can't seem to find his next move and blurts out, "I'm trapped. I can't play this game. I always lose. I'll never get into the final competition. I don't know why I even try." Ms. Valdez gently replies, "Yes, you're trapped all right. You're trapped in a bunch of thinking traps. I'm confident that you can find your next move but not until you jump out of these traps."

Ms. Valdez then explains to Gabriel that thinking traps are unhelpful patterns of thinking that we fall into: "When we fall into one of these thinking traps, we tend to feel very anxious, frustrated, and hopeless. But you can learn to jump out of a trap once you know when you've fallen into one." Ms. Valdez walks to the whiteboard and writes the most common thinking traps that cause people to feel anxious or depressed.

Name	Description	Example
Black-or-White	You think in black or white with no shades of gray.	"If I don't get an A+ in this class, then I'm a failure."
End of the World	You predict the worst and blow things out of proportion.	"I'll never get into college or have a successful career."
Filtering	You focus on negatives while ignoring positives of the situation.	"Yes, I got an A on the paper but still misspelled a word."
Fortune Telling	You think you can predict the future and typically predict the negative.	"I'm not going to get the part in the school play."
Mind Reading	You think you know what people think and why they do what they do.	"He's lying to let me down easy, but he really wants to break up."
Overgeneralization	You draw conclusions based on a single event or piece of evidence.	"I missed a dance step. I'm a horrible dancer."
Should, Must	You have ironclad rules that you think you and others should follow.	"I must get good grades." "He should be on time."
Doom and Gloom	You jump to negative conclusions before you have all the facts.	"They don't like me because they didn't invite me to the party."
Labeling	You put negative labels on yourself or on other people.	"I'm boring." "He's an idiot."
Fallacy of Fairness	You think that you know what's fair, but other people don't agree.	"It's not fair that she has a boyfriend and I don't."
Fallacy of Change	You think that you can change people if you pressure them enough.	"Although she said no, I'll get her to go with me to the prom."
Heaven's Reward	You think that your sacrifice will pay off someday.	"If I'm nice to her no matter how mean she is, one day she'll like me."
Being Right	You think you need to be right and you will go to any length to prove it.	"You don't know what you're talking about. The sky is green."
Personalization	You think that what people say or do is a reaction to you.	"It's all my fault that Julie didn't enjoy my birthday party."

for you to do

Look at the list of thinking traps and, on a blank sheet of paper, write the name of the thinking traps you tend to fall into. Then, write examples of your particular thinking traps next to each one. You can also download a blank copy of the My Thinking Traps Worksheet from http://www.newharbinger.com/49197.

My Thinking Traps Worksheet

Instructions: Circle the thinking traps that you most often fall into. Then, write your own example of each thinking trap.

Name	Description	Example	Your Example
Black-or-White	You think in black or white with no shades of gray.	"If I don't get an A+ in this class, then I'm a failure."	
End of the World	You predict the worst and blow things out of proportion.	"I'll never get into college or have a successful career."	
Filtering	You focus on negatives while ignoring positives of the situation.	"Yes, I got an A on the paper but still misspelled a word."	
Fortune Telling	You think you can predict the future and typically predict the negative.	"I'm not going to get the part in the school play."	
Mind Reading	You think you know what people think and why they do what they do.	"He's lying to let me down easy, but he really wants to break up."	
Overgeneralization	You draw conclusions based on a single event or piece of evidence.	"I missed a dance step. I'm a horrible dancer."	
Should, Must	You have ironclad rules that you think you and others should follow.	"I must get good grades." "He should be on time."	
Doom and Gloom	You jump to negative conclusions before you have all the facts.	"They don't like me because they didn't invite me to the party."	
Labeling	You put negative labels on yourself or on other people.	"I'm boring." "He's an idiot."	
Fallacy of Fairness	You think that you know what's fair, but other people don't agree.	"It's not fair that she has a boyfriend and that I don't."	
Fallacy of Change	You think that you can change people if you pressure them enough.	"Although she said no, I'll get her to go with me to the prom."	
Heavens Reward	You think that your sacrifice will pay off someday.	"If I'm nice to her no matter how mean she is one day she'll like me."	
Being Right	You think you need to be right and you will go to any length to prove it.	"You don't know what you're talking about. The sky is green."	
Personalization	You think that what people say or do is a reaction to you.	"It's all my fault that we lost the game."	

more to do

Write the thinking traps that cause you to feel overly anxious or down. Write any thinking traps you identified that surprised you.

Everyone has thinking traps. Describe the thinking traps of some of your friends and family members.

take another seat 5

for you to know

How you view or interpret events can create different feelings. One view of an event can make you feel anxious. Another view of the same event can make you feel sad. Still another view can make you feel happy—or at least not anxious or sad. Shifting your view of events can help you change the way you feel.

Asa was complaining to Ms. Iota, the theater arts teacher, that he kept stumbling over his lines—"I'll never get these lines down. I'm just not cut out to be an actor." Ms. Iota smiled and said that it depends on how you look at things. She then explained that where you sit in a theater gives you different views of the stage, and different views give you different experiences of the performance. If you're in the balcony, she said, you have one view of the stage and a particular experience of the performance. If you want a different experience of the performance, you might move to a different seat, perhaps to the front row of the orchestra section. "I wonder if going to a different spot in the theater of your mind might help you see things differently," she said. "Right now, from where you sit, you think that you're not cut out to be an actor because you keep stumbling over your lines. But what if you move to another seat and see it this way: Every actor stumbles over their lines at first, but that's part of the process. Actors keep at it, like you're doing, and with time, you'll stumble less." Asa considered this view and discovered that he felt less anxious and overwhelmed.

for you to do

You can learn to loosen your mind's grip on an interpretation of an event by teaching it to take another seat in the theater of your mind. You likely can view any situation from other perspectives if you try. Here are the steps:

Describe the event or situation:	
I keep stumbling over my lines.	
Describe the way you view or interpret the event or situation:	
It means that I'm not cut out to be an actor.	
Using a percentage, rate how strongly you believe the negative view is likely true:	90%
Rate how strongly anxious or sad this view makes you feel (on a scale of 0 to 10, where 10 is very anxious or sad):	8
Describe alternative views of the event or situation:	**Rate how strongly this view is likely true (0–100%)**
I'm stumbling over my lines because I'm a little anxious. All actors stumble over their lines at first. It's part of the process.	80%
I'm stumbling over my lines because I've never memorized this many lines before. I was given a bigger part with more lines because Ms. Iota believes I'm a good actor and can do this.	70%
I'm stumbling over my lines just like some other kids in the show and they're terrific actors.	90%
Re-rate how strongly (0–100%) you believe the negative view is true:	40%
Re-rate how strongly (0–10) anxious or sad this view makes you feel:	2

Now, you try it. Use the blank My Take Another Seat Worksheet on the next page or download a blank copy from http://www.newharbinger.com/49197.

My Take Another Seat Worksheet

Instructions: Describe the event or situation. Then, describe the way you view the event or situation (for example, what it means about you, about others, about the future). Rate how strongly (0 to 100% scale, where 100% is extremely strong) you believe this view is true. Then, rate how anxious or sad (0 to 10 scale, where 10 is very anxious or sad) this view makes you feel. Next, generate a list of alternative views and rate (0 to 100%, where 100% is highly likely) how likely each alternative is true and rate how anxious or sad (0 to 10 scale, where 10 is very anxious or sad) this view makes you feel. Last, **re-rate** how strongly you believe your first view is true and **re-rate** how anxious or sad this view makes you feel.

Describe the event or situation:	
Describe the way you view or interpret the event or situation:	
Using a percentage, rate how strongly you believe the negative view is likely true:	
Rate how strongly anxious or sad this view makes you feel (on a scale of 0 to 10, where 10 is very anxious or sad):	
Describe alternative views of the event or situation:	**Rate how strongly this view is likely true (0–100%)**
Re-rate how strongly (0–100%) you believe the negative view is true:	
Re-rate how strongly (0–10) anxious or sad this view makes you feel:	

Did the strength of your belief decrease as you considered different explanations or views of the event? What effect did that have on your feelings?

____

____

____

____

more to do

You might notice that your mind tends to view situations in the same way over and over. List the particular patterns of how you tend to view things that cause you to feel anxious or depressed.

____

____

____

Write several alternative views of these particular events or situations that could help you feel less anxious or depressed.

____

____

____

____

____

drink from the cup of optimism 6

for you to know

The attitude people have toward events affects how they feel about them. To feel less anxious and down, try drinking from the cup of optimism instead of the cup of pessimism.

Advik told Anja that he didn't want to go to a party on Saturday that their friends were attending. Anja asked Advik why he didn't want to go. Advik reeled off a list of negative thoughts. Anja laughed and said, "You'll feel better with a little attitude adjustment," and then helped Advik shift his attitude from negative to positive:

Negative Attitude	Positive Attitude
"What's the point, I won't enjoy myself."	"You always enjoy time with your friends. Try it."
"No one really wants me there. They won't even miss me."	"Your friends invited you, so they'll miss you if you're not there."
"I messed up my algebra final last week. I don't deserve to have a good time."	"You studied hard for the final. You deserve to reward yourself for your hard work."
"What if I don't know what to say?"	"These are your friends. You can talk to them."
"I'll die of embarrassment if no one speaks to me. I can't handle it."	"You probably won't do anything embarrassing, but even if you did, you can handle it."

Do you sometimes have thoughts like the ones Advik has? They're thoughts we all have sometimes. They're also not always based on the truth. Let's get started learning how you can reframe them based on what's actually true rather than what feels true.

for you to do

Draw a line connecting the positive attitude thoughts in the right column that would counter the negative attitude thoughts in the left column.

Negative Attitude Thoughts		Positive Attitude Thoughts
"Nothing ever works out for me."		"You have good friends who know you pretty well, and they like you."
"Once people get to know me, they won't like me."		"Although you might make a mistake because you're trying a new thing, it's not guaranteed. You've tried many new things, and they've worked out for you."
"I'm a total loser. I don't know why I even try."		"You're often nervous speaking with people, and no one seems to notice. Give yourself a break. Just because you're nervous doesn't make you weird."
"If they notice that I'm nervous, they'll think I'm weird."		"Most times things do work out okay for me. Let's see what really happens this time."
"If I try something new, I'll mess it up."		"Yes, days are hard for you, but things will get better. It's okay to go easy on yourself right now. That will make the days a little easier."
"Every day is impossible. I can't keep going."		"You lose sometimes, but this doesn't make you a loser. You try because you're not a loser."

more to do

Think of a situation that you feel anxious or depressed about. In the Negative Attitude section, write the negative thoughts you're having about the situation that make you feel especially anxious or depressed. In the Positive Attitude section, write more realistic, positive thoughts that could help you feel good rather than anxious or depressed.

Negative Attitude	Positive Attitude

Think of a situation recently in which you felt calm and happy. Write the positive thoughts that you were thinking that helped you feel calm and happy.

____

____

____

____

Imagine that same situation, and write several negative thoughts that would make you feel anxious and down.

____

____

____

____

Finally, list typical situations that make you anxious and depressed—situations in which you'd like to practice drinking from the cup of optimism.

____

____

____

____

____

____

7 handle hard knocks

for you to know

Hard knocks—moments when the outcomes of situations aren't what you hoped they'd be—are part of life. They also feel the worst in the moment, when the situation you're dealing with feels like the most important thing in the world. To feel less anxious and depressed, try transporting yourself into the future and then looking back.

Sophia is heartbroken. Tony, her boyfriend, just broke up with her. Sophia is depressed and at the same time she's terrified. She's convinced that she'll never find anyone as good as Tony. She's trying to hold it together when Ms. Barton, her English teacher, asks her why she's so upset. Sophia tells her about the breakup. Ms. Barton then says, "You know, we often feel the worst in the moment when what happened feels like the most important thing in the world. But transporting yourself into the future and then looking back at the event can help you feel better."

for you to do

Describe the event that upset you and then go through the following steps. It's great for situations like breakups, a poor grade on a test, an argument with a friend, an embarrassing moment, and other hard knocks of life. Use the blank My Handle Hard Knocks Worksheet below or download a copy from http://www.newharbinger.com/49197.

My Handle Hard Knocks Worksheet

Event that upset you: ____

____

____

Importance Scale

1	2	3	4	5	6	7	8	9	10
Couldn't care less				*Important, but not life changing*					*My life depends on this*

Rate how important this event feels before you start:	
Ask yourself the following questions and rate with the Importance Scale above:	
How important is this event at the moment?	
How important will this event be in an hour?	
How important will this event be in a day?	
How important will this event be in a week?	
How important will this event be in a month?	
How important will this event be in a year?	
How important will this event be in five years?	
How important will this event be in ten years?	
Re-rate how important this event feels after you finish:	

more to do

Describe what it was like to get out of the moment and look at the event with the perspective of time.

___

___

___

___

List other hard knocks you might have some day that this activity might help you handle.

___

___

___

___

Now that you know that, as they say, "time heals all wounds," describe how you feel about other hard knocks you've experienced in the past, and the hard knocks you might experience in the future.

___

___

___

___

___

8 reset predictions

for you to know

How you feel often depends on the predictions you make about the future. When you're anxious, you tend to predict something bad will happen. When you're sad, you tend to predict that nothing will turn out right for you or that you can't do something because you feel too down to do it. You can feel less anxious and less sad by learning to reset your predictions.

One day, when Marisol was feeling very anxious and sad, she noticed something interesting about her thinking. She tended to predict one negative thing after another, but the predictions almost never came true. If she was feeling anxious about a party, she noticed she predicted that she would make a fool of herself, but in fact, she made a couple of new friends. If she was feeling sad, she noticed that she predicted she wouldn't enjoy herself at all, but when she went, she did enjoy herself a little. Marisol decided to test her predictions, instead of assuming they were true. After a few weeks, she noticed that she was feeling less anxious and depressed.

for you to do

A simple way to reset predictions is to test the accuracy of the predictions you're making when you're feeling anxious or depressed. Because you tend to see the future in a particular way, you might not often stop to ask yourself two important questions: "What is the prediction I'm making?" and "How likely is this prediction to be true?" Sometimes simply realizing the degree to which your predictions are inaccurate may be enough to change your tendency to predict the future in negative ways.

For the next two weeks, every time you predict a negative outcome, such as losing a friend or not enjoying an activity *at all*, record the prediction on the worksheet below or download a blank copy from http://www.newharbinger.com/49197. Then, indicate how strongly you believe the prediction is true (0 to 100%, where 100% means that you believe the prediction is completely true) and what really happened. If your prediction is false, place a check mark by it. Here's how Marisol completed her worksheet.

What negative event did you predict?	How likely is prediction true?	What really happened?	Prediction false?
No one will speak to me at the party.	80%	My friends spoke to me and a couple of new girls said hi.	✓
I won't have any fun hanging out with Jenny.	75%	I had some fun, more than I thought I would.	✓
I won't know what to say.	80%	I was quiet at first, but once I was comfortable I had plenty to say.	✓

My Reset Predictions Worksheet

Instructions: For the next two weeks, every time you predict a negative outcome, such as someone getting upset with you or not enjoying an activity ***at all***, write the negative prediction. Then, rate how strongly you believe the prediction is true (0 to 100%, where 100% means that you believe the prediction is completely true). Last, write what really happened. If your prediction was false, place a check (✓) mark by it.

What negative event did you predict?	How likely is prediction true?	What really happened?	Prediction false?

List the kinds of predictions you tend to make and describe how they make you feel. Do you make more anxious predictions than depressed predictions, or vice versa?

Think back over the last few months and ask yourself how often the predictions you made were true and how often they were false. Describe how this makes you feel.

more to do

Now that you have a better understanding of the kinds of predictions you tend to make that cause you to feel anxious and depressed, list the events or activities coming up in the next few weeks or months that might make you feel anxious or depressed. What are the predictions you're likely to make? How likely is it that these predictions will be true?

For predictions that aren't likely to be true, describe why you think they're not likely to be true. How are you feeling now about these future events?

jump back from doom and gloom 9

for you to know

When you overestimate the likelihood of something bad happening or underestimate your ability to handle bad events, you've likely jumped into doom and gloom. You can decrease your anxious and depressed feelings by learning to jump back from doom and gloom and see events and yourself realistically.

Andres was freaking out about his bass solo in the upcoming school concert. He told Mr. Tejeda, his music teacher, that he might skip the concert because he wasn't feeling well. Mr. Tejeda could see that Andres was nervous and told him that he might feel less anxious and down if he answered three questions.

First, Mr. Tejeda asked Andres, "What's the worst that could happen if you played the solo?" Andres said that the worst thing would be forgetting the music. Mr. Tejeda said that it would help to consider how likely it was that this would happen. "For example," Mr. Tejeda said, "you've never forgotten a solo in the past, not even music that was longer and more complicated than this." Andres agreed and added that he'd rehearsed this music more than any other solo he'd ever played.

Mr. Tejeda then asked, "What's the best that could happen?" Andres told him that the best is that he would remember and play every note of the music perfectly. Andres laughed at this and told Mr. Tejeda that he didn't think this was very likely.

Finally, Mr. Tejeda asked, "What's the most likely thing that could happen?" Andres told Mr. Tejeda that most likely he would remember the music and miss a few notes. Mr. Tejeda then asked, "And how bad would that be?" Andres smiled and said that it wouldn't be horrible, certainly not as horrible as it felt before he answered the questions.

for you to do

Make as many copies of the blank My Jump Back from Doom and Gloom Worksheet below as you need (or download several blank copies of the worksheet from http://www.newharbinger.com/49197).

Now, think about something that causes you to feel anxious or depressed when you think about doing it and go through the steps in the worksheet.

My Jump Back from Doom and Gloom Worksheet

Instructions: Think about something that makes you feel very anxious or depressed when you think about doing it. Then, in the space below, write the worst you can imagine happening and circle the probability or likelihood in percentage that the worst thing will happen. Repeat this for the other two questions. Last, rate how bad it would be if the most likely thing actually happened (0–10, where 10 is end-of-the-world bad).

What's the worst that could happen?										
How likely is it that the worst will actually happen?										
0%	10%	20%	30%	40%	50%	60%	70%	80%	90%	100%
What's the best that could happen?										
How likely is it that the best will actually happen?										
0%	10%	20%	30%	40%	50%	60%	70%	80%	90%	100%
What's the most likely to happen?										
How likely is it that the most likely will actually happen?										
0%	10%	20%	30%	40%	50%	60%	70%	80%	90%	100%
How bad would that be for you?										
0	1	2	3	4	5	6	7	8	9	10

Describe what it was like for you to answer the three questions. Did the level of your anxious and depressed feelings change as you went through the three questions? Did your confidence increase or decrease as you answered the questions?

____

____

____

____

____

____

more to do

Another way to jump back from doom and gloom is to think through how to handle the most likely worst outcome if it happened. Mr. Tejeda asked Andres how he would handle missing a few notes of the music during his solo. Andres said that he'd get his mind off it with schoolwork and hanging out with friends. He might even learn a new and better solo. He'd also remind himself that everyone makes mistakes and that he has bounced back from bigger mistakes than missing a few notes. He'd also speak to his bandmates and Mr. Tejeda. They know what it's like to mess up a performance.

Now, you try it. Use the worksheet provided or download a blank copy of the My Jump Back from Doom and Gloom Coping Plan from http://www.newharbinger.com/49197.

My Jump Back from Doom and Gloom Coping Plan

Instructions: Write the most likely worst prediction and rate how confident you are that you can handle the prediction if it happens. Then, answer the following questions and re-rate how confident you are that you can handle the prediction if it happened.

Describe the most likely worst prediction:	
Confidence I can handle this (0–100%):	
What are my strengths that will help me cope?	
What can I do to help me cope?	
What can I say to myself that will help me cope?	
From whom can I seek support to help me cope?	
Confidence I can handle this (0–100%):	

Describe what it was like to think through how you would handle the most likely worst case scenario. Did you feel less doom and gloom?

overthrow the tyranny of should 10

for you to know

"Should" statements can increase your anxious and depressed feelings. Thinking you "should" do something increases the pressure you feel to get it done. Thinking that you "should have" done something causes you to feel needlessly guilty and bad about yourself. Learning to change "should" statements is a quick way to feel less anxious and depressed.

Cornell used to tell himself a hundred times a day that he "should" do something: "I should be nicer to my friends," "I should have known better," "I should have studied more for the quiz," "I should feel happy even when I don't." One day Mr. Franklin, Cornell's AP history teacher, asked Cornell to stay after class. Mr. Franklin had noticed that Cornell wasn't himself and asked him how he was feeling. Cornell told Mr. Franklin that he was super stressed and upset with himself—"I should have studied harder for the last history test. I thought I knew the material about Henry VIII, but I should have known better than to trust my gut."

Mr. Franklin interrupted Cornell and said, "You just learned about Henry VIII, one of the worst tyrants of the sixteenth century. He told people what to do and they did it or else. They didn't have a choice. When you do something just because you think you 'should,' you serve the 'should' tyrant. Life in a tyranny is hard. People feel more stressed, more anxious, and more down. But when you take charge of your choices, you take charge of your life. That's when you'll start to feel less anxious and bad about yourself."

for you to do

To overthrow the tyranny of "should," Cornell took charge of his choices by deciding whether he'd do something or not by examining what he'd lose or gain. Then he stepped back and decided what he wanted to do and why.

<table>
<tr><th colspan="2">Write the should you want to overthrow:</th></tr>
<tr><td colspan="2">I should study another two hours, but it's late and I'm so tired.</td></tr>
<tr><th>What you lose:</th><th>What you gain:</th></tr>
<tr><td>Sleep! I'm so tired in class that I'm missing important stuff.</td><td>More sleep and less stress. I might be able to study less if I'm fully alert and awake in my classes.</td></tr>
<tr><th colspan="2">Restate as a desire, wish or want:</th></tr>
<tr><td colspan="2">I want to go to bed now so that I'm alert in my classes tomorrow. That's the best way to do well in school.</td></tr>
</table>

First, make a list of the "shoulds" that tend to run through your mind that cause you to feel anxious or depressed. They're likely about the kind of friend, student, athlete, son or daughter, you believe you "should" be.

____

____

____

____

____

____

Now, use the blank My Overthrow the Tyranny of Should Worksheet on the next page, or download the worksheet from http://www.newharbinger.com/49197.

My Overthrow the Tyranny of Should Worksheet

Instructions: First, write the ***should*** you want to overthrow (for example, "I should be on time."). Next, write what you lose and gain if you decide to do that (for example, "Be on time"). Last, restate the ***should*** as a want (for example, "I want to be on time").

Write the should you want to overthrow:	
What you lose:	**What you gain:**
Restate as a desire, wish or want:	

more to do

Go back to the "shoulds" you listed. Which "should" statements make you feel the most anxious, guilty, or down? Why?

____

____

____

____

____

Describe what you fear might happen if you overthrow the tyranny of "shoulds." Are you afraid that, if you let go of "shoulds," you'll become lazy or won't do as well in school or in sports? Are you afraid that, if you let go of "shoulds," you'll become a bad person?

____

____

____

____

____

____

try imperfection for a change 11

for you to know

Perfection is theoretically possible but not practically possible. Therefore, striving for perfection means you chronically fail. It doesn't matter how smart you are or how hard you work—when you strive for perfection, anything you accomplish can always be better. Striving for perfection undermines your self-confidence and increases your anxious and depressed feelings.

Shanice is an excellent student, a good friend, and a pole vaulter on the track and field team. Shanice is also a perfectionist. Although she has nearly all As, she's very anxious about her grades. Although she's a good friend, she often feels intensely guilty when she is a little impatient with her friends. On the surface, Shanice's life looks great, but on the inside, Shanice feels anxious, guilty, frustrated, and sad.

One day at practice, Shanice threw the pole to the side after she missed the jump. Coach Wilson asked her how she was doing, and she told him that she was thinking of changing her sport: "No matter how hard I try, I can't make it past sixteen feet."

Coach Wilson then told Shanice a story: Imagine two pole vaulters standing at the line. They're both strong and experienced vaulters. Pole vaulter A tells the judge to place the pole at 16 feet. However, vaulter A's best vault is 14 feet. As vaulter A looks at the pole, she knows that the pole is set two feet higher than her best jump. She feels very anxious because she's not confident that she can vault 16 feet. In fact, she knows that there's little chance she'll make the 16-foot jump. She's hesitating because in her mind she's already missed the jump. She knows that no matter how hard she tries, she's going to fail because the goal is unrealistic. When she fails, and she will fail, she feels sad and bad about herself.

Pole vaulter B's best jump is also 14 feet. However, vaulter B tells the judge to set the pole at 14 feet and half an inch. As vaulter B looks at the pole, she thinks, "It's just half an inch higher than my record. It's within reach." Vaulter B feels a reasonable level of anxiety because she's confident that 14 feet and half an inch is achievable. In her mind, she can see herself making the jump. She doesn't hesitate. She bolts off the line because she believes she has a chance. Even if vaulter B misses the jump, she'll be close. That's because she set a reasonable goal. She'll want to try again, and she will try again.

Shanice listened as Coach Wilson added, "Nothing succeeds like success, and nothing lowers the likelihood of success than striving for an unrealistic goal. Perfection is an unachievable standard, and striving for perfection is an unrealistic goal. Why don't you start to strive for excellence, which is an achievable standard, rather than perfection?"

for you to do

There's nothing wrong with having high standards for yourself. Excellence is a high standard. Perfection, on the other hand, is an impossible standard, and striving for perfection can create a lot of anxiety and depression for you. To see if you're striving for perfection, circle Yes or No to answer the following questions:

Do you often feel depressed, frustrated, or anxious about your performance?	Yes	No	Do you agonize over small details (for example, what movie to rent)?	Yes	No
Do you often criticize yourself for not doing a good enough job?	Yes	No	Do you excessively check your work for mistakes?	Yes	No
Do you often spend a lot of time and effort on tasks that others do more quickly and easily?	Yes	No	Do you make long, overly detailed to do lists?	Yes	No
Do you chronically procrastinate on tasks, even small ones?	Yes	No	Do you spend a lot of time on tasks because you're too thorough?	Yes	No
Do you often have trouble completing tasks or give up easily?	Yes	No	Are you very hard on yourself about small mistakes?	Yes	No

Look at your answers. Do you think you strive for perfection or excellence? Describe what it was like to think through your answers.

____

____

____

____

____

____

Describe how your life might look different if you were to strive for excellence rather than perfection, and why.

____

____

____

____

____

____

more to do

Compromising is setting more realistic standards or being more flexible with your very high standards. For example, if you believe that making even a single mistake during a class presentation is unacceptable, you'll likely overprepare and spend five hours preparing the presentation. You might rehearse the presentation hour after hour, or spend hours memorizing the presentation so that you don't make any mistakes.

The first step in compromising is to ask yourself, "What level of imperfection am I willing to tolerate?" For perfectionists, compromising their standards can be scary, so it helps to lower your standards gradually, in steps. For example, the first step to more reasonable standards in the above example might involve spending three hours instead of five preparing for a presentation. Once you're comfortable lowering your standards a bit, lower them some more. For example, the next step might involve spending two hours preparing for the next presentation, and then spending one hour preparing for the presentation after that.

Now, you try it. On the blank worksheet, write an unrealistic standard and how you try to achieve the unrealistic standard (for example, studying for five hours, rereading an email for typos twenty times). Then, write the steps you'll follow to compromise a little. You can also download a copy from http://www.newharbinger.com/49197.

My Try Imperfection for a Change Worksheet

Instructions: In the table below, write an ***unrealistic standard*** and ***how you try to achieve the unrealistic standard*** (for example, studying for five hours, rereading an email for typos twenty times). Then, write the steps you'll follow to compromise a little.

Unrealistic Standard	
How I Try to Achieve the Unrealistic Standard	
How I Can Learn to Compromise a Little	
Step 1:	
Step 2:	
Step 3:	
Step 4:	
Step 5:	

Describe what it was like to compromise your perfectionistic standards.

see the gray to feel better 12

for you to know

People who feel very anxious or depressed tend to view things in extremes. It's either black or it's white. Extreme views tend to create extreme feelings. However, events and people aren't that simple. Learning to see events and yourself in shades of gray rather than in black and white can lessen your anxious and depressed feelings.

Aniyah is a great student and a top-notch soccer player, but she tends to see things in black and white. If she gets a B on a test, she thinks, "I'm stupid." If she misses a pass, she thinks, "I'm useless." If she loses her cool with a friend, she thinks, "I'm a horrible friend." Aniyah's tendency to see things in black and white causes her to feel very anxious or depressed at school, with friends and family, and on the soccer field.

for you to do

Think of ten people you know (coworkers, family members, friends, teachers) and write their names on the 100% to 0% line where you think they belong for each category. Then, write your name on the line where you think you belong for each category. You can also download a blank My See the Gray to Feel Better Worksheet from http://www.newharbinger.com/49197.

My See the Gray to Feel Better Worksheet

Instructions: Think of ten people you know (coworkers, family members, friends, teachers) and write their names on the scale where you think they belong for each category. Then, write your name on the scale where you think you belong for each category.

Qualities of a Friend		
100% ----------------------- 50% ----------------------- 0%		
Drops everything to help. Never upset, always patient, calm. Always does what others want.	Helps when possible, considers others. Usually calm, sometimes argues. Usually thinks about others.	Never helps, no matter what. Always upset, argues, too sensitive. Only thinks of self, self-centered.
Qualities of a Student		
100% ----------------------- 50% ----------------------- 0%		
Never takes breaks from studying. Always gets As on tests and work. Loved by every teacher.	Balances studying with fun. Good grades, but not perfect. Liked by most teachers.	Never studies or does school work. Fails every test, quiz, assignment. Sometimes frustrating to teachers.
Qualities of an Athlete or Performer		
100% ----------------------- 50% ----------------------- 0%		
Always practicing without a break. Best rank in school, state, country. Never given critical feedback.	Balances practicing with fun. Good ranking, but not the best. Sometimes given critical feedback.	Never practices even a minute. Worst in school, state, country. Always given critical feedback.

Qualities of a Family Member		
100% ----------	50% ----------	---------- 0%
Always thinks of family first. Never upset with family members. Gets along with everyone in family.	Thinks about self and family. Sometimes upset with family. Usually gets along with family.	Never thinks about family first. Always upset with family members. Doesn't ever get along with family.

Describe what you learned from this exercise and how it affected your anxious and depressed feelings.

____

____

____

____

____

Which categories were the most difficult to place your name in the gray or middle area rather than the extremes of the category? Why do you think that is?

____

____

____

____

more to do

Words like "always" or "never" are signs of black-and-white thinking. For example, if you once gave a poor class presentation, you may think to yourself, "I always mess up presentations."

Write three examples of "always" or "never" statements you make about yourself as a family member, friend, student, and athlete or performer.

1. ______________________________

____

2. ______________________________

____

3. ______________________________

____

Now, replace the "always" or "never" statements with more realistic gray statements. For example, rather than "I always mess up class presentations," write "I sometimes mess up class presentations."

1. ______________________________

____

2. ______________________________

____

3. ______________________________

____

de-magnify to de-stress 13

for you to know

When people are anxious or depressed, they tend to magnify details of a situation and lose sight of the bigger picture. Magnifying the consequences of an event, such as what happens if you don't do well on a test, can cause you to feel very stressed and anxious. Magnifying the importance of events can cause you to feel depressed and overwhelmed. Learning to de-magnify not only helps you to feel less anxious, but it can also help you to feel less depressed.

Tiara was feeling anxious and depressed after an argument with Deja, her best friend. Ms. Harvey noticed that something was bothering Tiara and asked what it was. Tiara began to cry and told Ms. Harvey about the argument with Deja and that she was certain she'd lost her best friend. Ms. Harvey told Tiara that she might be magnifying the argument, and it might help to look at the bigger picture when it came to her relationship with Deja. Ms. Harvey reminded Tiara that she and Deja often argued but always made up. They'd been through tough times together and depended on each other. Ms. Harvey added that sometimes Tiara apologized first and sometimes Deja did, but they always worked it out.

for you to do

Magnifying an event is like looking at the event through the magnifying end of binoculars. It makes the event look bigger than it really is. To de-magnify an event, try looking at the event through the other end of the binoculars. This means you step back and see the bigger picture.

Make a copy of the blank My De-Magnify to De-Stress Worksheet below or download a blank copy from http://www.newharbinger.com/49197.

My De-Magnify to De-Stress Worksheet

Instructions: In the box on the left, describe an event that's causing you to feel anxious or depressed. If you're feeling anxious, it's likely about an event that's approaching. If you're feeling depressed, it's likely about an event that occurred in the past. Describe the event as if you're looking through the magnifying end of binoculars in as much detail as possible. In the box on the right, describe the same event as if you're looking through the other (de-magnifying) end of the binoculars so that you can see the bigger picture.

Magnified View	De-Magnified View

more to do

Describe the difference in how you felt when you looked through the magnifying and then the de-magnifying end of the binoculars. Did you feel more or less anxious or down?

____

____

____

Look at other examples of magnifying and de-magnifying events. Circle how anxious or depressed you feel (where *H* is high, *M* is medium, and *L* is low) when you view the event through the magnified and then the de-magnified end of the binoculars.

Event: Failed a math test.			
Magnified View		**De-Magnified View**	
I'm going to fail the math class and fail out of school.	*H* *M* *L*	I have a B average in math and good grades in my other classes.	*H* *M* *L*
Event: Argument with best friend.			
Magnified View		**De-Magnified View**	
I've lost the best friend I'll ever have in my life.	*H* *M* *L*	We've had arguments before but we've always made up.	*H* *M* *L*

Event: Missed a shot during the big game.			
Magnified View		**De-Magnified View**	
Coach will bench me for life, and I'll never play basketball again.	*H* *M* *L*	Coach doesn't bench a player for life because of one missed shot.	*H* *M* *L*
Event: Dropped lunch tray in the cafeteria.			
Magnified View		**De-Magnified View**	
Everyone thinks I'm a nerd..	*H* *M* *L*	Dropping a tray doesn't mean I'm a nerd.	*H* *M* *L*
Event: Played wrong note during school holiday concert.			
Magnified View		**De-Magnified View**	
I ruined the holiday concert.	*H* *M* *L*	Everyone applauded, and kids and parents said I played well.	*H* *M* *L*
Event: Parents grounded me Saturday night.			
Magnified View		**De-Magnified View**	
My parents grounded me for the weekend. I'll lose all my friends.	*H* *M* *L*	All my friends texted me Saturday night and told me that they missed me.	*H* *M* *L*

Describe what it was like for you to shift from a magnified view of an event to a de-magnified view.

14 slice the responsibility pie

for you to know

Taking more responsibility than you deserve for a bad outcome can make you feel very anxious, guilty, or depressed. Learning to take a slice of responsibility for the way something turns out but not to take on the whole pie can help lessen these feelings.

Tiana's boyfriend, Zion, broke up with her and she's devastated. She's convinced that it's all her fault, even though her friends tell her that Zion wasn't so great. Tiana has never felt as depressed as she feels now. She can't sleep and she can't eat, and all she can think about are the things she did wrong. Sunday afternoon Tiana and her mom are baking a pie when her mom notices Tiana is crying. Her mom asks her what upset her, and Tiana tells her mom about the breakup and that it's all her fault. Tiana's mother tells her that life is complicated and that events, like pies, can be sliced in more than one way. "You're not the whole pie." she added. "You're just one slice among many. You weren't the only one who caused things to go the way they went, even if it feels that way right now."

for you to do

To slice the responsibility pie, think of an upsetting event that made you feel anxious, sad, or guilty, and then follow the steps below. Use the blank My Slice the Responsibility Pie Worksheet below or download a blank copy from http://www.newharbinger.com/49197.

My Slice the Responsibility Pie Worksheet

Instructions: Describe an upsetting event that feels like it's all your fault. Rate how strongly you believe that the event is your fault (0 to 100%, where 100% means you believe it completely). Then, rate how sad or guilty you feel now (0 to 10, where 10 is extreme). List as many factors as you can think of that may have contributed to the upsetting event. Next, go down the list and assign each factor a percentage amount representing how much you estimate each factor contributed to the event. Include yourself as the final factor and assign yourself a percentage amount. Finally, review all the factors and their percentages of responsibility. Be sure the total percentage across all the factors you listed adds up to 100%. Re-rate how sad or guilty you feel now (0 to 10, where 10 is extreme).

Upsetting Event:	
How strongly do you believe that the upsetting event is your fault?	
How sad or guilty do you feel?	
Factor that may have contributed to event:	**% Contribution**
Total	
Now how strongly do you believe that the upsetting event is your fault?	
Now how sad or guilty do you feel?	

Here's how Tiana completed the worksheet:

Upsetting Event:	Zion broke up with me because I shouted at him sometimes.
How strongly do you believe that the upsetting event is your fault?	90%
How sad or guilty do you feel?	9
Factor that may have contributed to event:	**% Contribution**
Zion is going through a lot because of his parents' divorce.	50%
His parents fight all the time and that upsets Zion.	20%
Zion is stressed about his college applications.	10%
Chloe has been talking trash about me to Zion.	5%
Zion has been unhappy about a lot of stuff, not just our relationship.	10%
I shouted at Zion sometimes when he yelled at me.	5%
Total	100%
Now how strongly do you believe that the upsetting event is your fault?	20%
Now how sad or guilty do you feel?	3

Do you think slicing the responsibility pie helped you feel less sad or guilty? Why?

Make a list of other events that you thought were all your fault and try slicing the responsibility pie for those.

more to do

Slicing the responsibility pie doesn't just help you feel less sad or guilty about past events. It can help you feel less anxious about future events too. When you take on too much responsibility for an outcome, such as winning a big game or whether you get into college or not, you can feel a lot of pressure to win the game or get into college. Fortunately, slicing the responsibility pie can help redistribute the responsibility you feel to other factors. This will help you see that you alone are not responsible for the outcome, which will decrease the pressure and anxiety you feel.

Identify an event or situation coming up that's making you anxious. For example, perhaps you're anxious about a soccer game you're playing on Saturday. Here's how to slice the responsibility pie. First, there are eleven players on your soccer team, including you. That means that you share the responsibility of winning or losing with ten other team members. Then there's the weather, the referees (perhaps one is having a bad day), and whether the field is in good shape or not.

Now, just like you learned, slice the responsibility pie for the upcoming event that's making you anxious. Brainstorm as many factors as you can think of here, and then distribute the responsibility in a worksheet.

____

____

____

____

____

____

____

How did you feel before and after?

____

____

____

You can slice the responsibility pie to decrease your anger too. Was it really all that other player's fault you lost the game? Was it really all your teacher's fault that you didn't do well on the quiz? Describe a time when you were feeling angry and slice the responsibility pie. What did you notice? Describe how slicing the responsibility pie might help you feel less angry when things don't go your way.

____

____

____

____

____

____

____

15 breathe slowly and deeply

for you to know

Whether you're anxious or depressed, slow deep breathing can soothe, relax, and center you. Breathing slowly and deeply is easy to learn and helps counter the tendency to breathe quickly and shallowly when you're stressed, anxious, or down.

Breathing is automatic, but automatic breathing is not always relaxed breathing. Relaxed breathing is slow and deep because you breathe with your abdominal muscles. With each breath in, your abdominal muscles rise. With each breath out, your abdominal muscles fall. Stressed or tense breathing, on the other hand, is quick and shallow. When you're anxious, you breathe with the upper part of your chest, throat, and nose. Slow and deep abdominal breathing is one of the best ways to release stress and tension in the body. That's because slow, deep breaths send a signal to your brain to relax. The brain then sends this same signal to your body—a signal to relax, release, and let go. Your heart rate slows, your blood pressure decreases, and your muscles relax as you breathe slowly and deeply. Chest breathing, on the other hand, is more likely to keep you in a stressed-out, anxious, or agitated state.

for you to do

In this activity, you'll practice the 4-7-8 breathing technique. This involves inhaling for four seconds, holding the breath for seven seconds, and exhaling for eight seconds. And it trains your body to breathe slowly and deeply. To practice 4-7-8 breathing, get comfortable in a favorite chair or lie on your bed, uncross your legs and arms, and close your eyes. (Audio for the 4-7-8 breathing technique is available at http://www.newharbinger.com/49197.)

1. Place one hand on your upper chest and the other hand just below your ribcage. This allows you to feel your diaphragm move as you breathe in and out.
2. Close your mouth and say to yourself the word ***EASY*** as you breathe in slowly through your nose as you count ***1-2-3-4*** slowly to yourself. Imagine the word ***EASY*** as you slowly inhale. Feel your stomach move out against your hand as you slowly inhale. Imagine your breath is going all the way down into your stomach and filling it up.
3. Hold your breath now and slowly count ***1-2-3-4-5-6-7*** in your head.
4. Next, say the word ***CALM*** to yourself and imagine the word in your mind's eye as you exhale through pursed lips and slowly count ***1-2-3-4-5-6-7-8***. Let your breath make a ***whoosh*** sound as you exhale. As you breathe, imagine the air traveling in and out of your lungs slowly and evenly.
5. Take another slow, deep breath in through your nose as you imagine the word ***EASY*** and count slowly to 4. Hold your breath as you slowly count to 7. Then say to yourself ***CALM*** and exhale as you slowly count to 8. Pause for a moment, then again: inhale ***EASY*** *1-2-3-4,* hold *1-2-3-4-5-6-7,* then exhale ***CALM*** *1-2-3-4-5-6-7-8.* Pause for a moment, then again: inhale ***EASY*** *1-2-3-4,* hold *1-2-3-4-5-6-7,* exhale ***CALM*** *1-2-3-4-5-6-7-8.*

Repeat this slow, deep, and rhythmic flow for a total of ten to fifteen minutes. If your mind wanders during the exercise, just refocus your attention on the picture of the word EASY or CALM in your mind's eye. Continue breathing in and out, noticing your abdomen rise and fall.

more to do

Now that you've learned the 4-7-8 breathing technique, think of some situations in which you could use it to relax. Circle any of the following situations that tend to make you feel anxious or stressed:

Taking an exam	Friends pressuring you to take sides
Going on a date	Hearing your parents argue
Speaking with a teacher	Hanging out at a party
Performing in a recital or game	Doing homework
Taking your driver's test	Arguing with your best friend
Doing something for the first time	Flying on a plane

Now, in the space below, list events or situations in which you often feel anxious or stressed—either from the list above, or ones that don't appear in the list but tend to repeatedly happen to you. Close your eyes, imagine one of these situations, and rate your anxiety or stress level on a scale from 0 to 10 (0 being completely relaxed and 10 being highly anxious or stressed). Place that number by the event or situation below. Then, practice slow, deep breathing for five minutes and re-rate your anxiety or stress level:

Imagined Stressful Event or Situation	Stress Level *Before*	Stress Level *After*

Describe what it was like to imagine a stressful situation and to breathe slowly and deeply. How quickly did you feel relaxed and calm? What else did you learn that was helpful?

____

____

____

Bend and breathe is another quick breathing technique. It's a great way to clear your head, relax your body, and boost your energy. (Audio for this technique is available for download at http://www.newharbinger.com/49197.) Try it when you first get out of bed in the morning:

1. Stand and slowly bend forward from the waist, with your knees slightly bent. Let your arms dangle close to the floor.
2. Inhale slowly and deeply as you slowly roll your body up to a standing position, lifting your head last.
3. Hold your breath for just a few seconds in this standing position.
4. Exhale slowly as you return to the original position, bending forward from the waist.

Describe how you felt at the end of the exercise. Did you feel a bit more alert? Did you feel a bit more relaxed?

____

____

____

____

16 slip into the present moment

for you to know

Anxiety and worry are about the future. You repeatedly think about something bad that could happen but isn't happening now. Depression is about the past. You repeatedly think about something bad that happened in the past, although there's nothing you can do about it now. Slipping into the present moment places your thinking in the present where you can see things as they truly are.

Denzel felt anxious and depressed a lot. He always had something on his mind. He worried that his girlfriend was going to dump him when she didn't return his texts immediately. He worried that his boss was going to fire him from the ice cream shop where he worked because he tended to get confused when making change for customers. He dwelled on things when they hadn't worked out or he thought they hadn't worked out. One day, Denzel told Ms. Demorest, his health education teacher, that he felt like nothing went his way. Ms. Demorest said Denzel's life might feel better if he spent more time in the present moment rather than in the future or the past.

for you to do

Mindfulness is a way to slip into the present moment. *Mindfulness* is being aware of yourself, your actions, and your surroundings in the present moment. For busy people, one of the best ways to practice mindfulness is to be mindful while you're doing an activity. In a mindful activity, you observe every detail of the experience. It doesn't matter what activity you choose to practice mindfulness with, so long as it's brief, you can do it every day, and there are opportunities to pay attention to your senses (sight, smell, taste, touch, sound) while you do the activity. For example, to engage your five senses as you walk from the front door to the kitchen, first focus on the smells of your house. Then, observe the pattern in the carpet or drapes. Feel the weight beneath your feet and the sound you make walking across the carpet or floor. Pay attention to where you place your keys or lunch bag and the sounds they make as you drop them there. At first, you may wish to start an activity by paying attention to one sense (for example, what you see in the moment), then adding other senses (smell, taste, touch, sound) as you get better at mindful activity.

Circle any of the activities below that you could do mindfully using your five senses:

Combing your hair	Washing dishes	Eating a snack or lunch
Applying nail polish	Walking to school or the bus	Drinking a glass of water
Washing your face	Vacuuming your room	Tying your shoes
Brushing your teeth	Walking up the stairs	Putting on a shirt
Taking a shower or bath	Bouncing a ball	Jogging or running
Coloring or drawing	Washing the car	Folding your clothes

Now think through a typical day. Find an activity to practice in a mindful way, perhaps one from the list above. In the table below, write the activity that you plan to practice doing mindfully, and when you'll do it. Next to the activity, circle the senses to which you'll pay particular attention. For example, you'll certainly want to pay attention to taste if your mindful activity is eating.

Activity	Senses				
	Sight	Sound	Touch	Taste	Smell
	Sight	Sound	Touch	Taste	Smell
	Sight	Sound	Touch	Taste	Smell
	Sight	Sound	Touch	Taste	Smell
	Sight	Sound	Touch	Taste	Smell
	Sight	Sound	Touch	Taste	Smell

more to do

What activity did you try to do mindfully? How difficult was it to slip into the present moment when doing this activity?

____

____

____

Which senses best grounded you in the present moment?

____

____

Which senses grounded you the least?

____

____

When you were able to slip into the present moment, what did you notice? Did you feel differently? Describe the feelings and what you learned.

____

____

____

____

____

Doing several things at the same time is the opposite of mindful activity. What things do you tend to do at the same time (for example, listening to music while eating your breakfast, talking on the phone while walking to class)?

____

____

____

____

____

____

The next time you find yourself doing these activities, see if you can do them mindfully, one at a time. Notice if that makes a difference in how you feel while you're doing them.

17 slow the mental merry-go-round

for you to know

Whether you're anxious or depressed, you likely ride the mental merry-go-round. Your mind goes round and round. You think over and over that you're stupid or a loser because you made a little mistake. You lie awake in bed at night as you think about a problem over and over and what you can do to fix it. As your mind goes round and round, you feel more anxious or more down until you want to get off the mental merry-go-round but you don't know how. To get off the mental merry-go-round, start by learning to slow it down.

Rudra knows that he's a worrier, and once his mind starts to go round and round, he's powerless to stop it. He worries about tests, about his friendships, about his family, even about his health. One day, Rudra's older sister, Sabrin, noticed that Rudra was upset and asked what was going on with him. Rudra told her that he couldn't stop worrying, and he was exhausted and frustrated with himself. Sabrin listened and said, "That's the mental merry-go-round. I get stuck on that ride too sometimes. I learned a trick from the school counselor to slow the ride down." Sabrin then described how to do it: you choose specific times to worry and only worry during those times. After Rudra tried it for week, he felt less stressed. Although it was still difficult to stop worrying, he was getting better at slowing it down a little.

for you to do

One way to slow the mental merry-go-round is to learn to postpone worrying about a big event that's weeks away, such as a presentation you're giving in English class, or dwelling on a negative event in the past, such as an upsetting conversation with a friend. Follow these steps to slow the mental merry-go-round:

Step 1: Select several times each day to worry or dwell on events or problems. Make the times convenient and not too close to bedtime—for example, 8:00 a.m., 11:00 a.m., 1:00 p.m., 4:00 p.m., and 7:00 p.m.

Step 2: Decide where you'll worry or dwell. Find a place where you don't spend much time (not in your bedroom, for example), and use this place only for worrying about or dwelling on events or problems. This place then becomes linked to the mental merry-go-round and not linked to your bedroom, for example.

Step 3: Decide how much time you'll worry or dwell. Set a minimum of ten minutes.

Step 4: As soon as you become aware that you're worrying or dwelling, remind yourself that you'll have time to think about it later, during your next worry or dwelling period, and there's no need to think about it now. Tell yourself that it's better to deal with the situation during the next worry or dwelling period than right now because the situation will have your full attention during the period you set aside for it. Write down the worries or thoughts so that you remember them. You may wish to carry a small notebook to write down worries or thoughts as they occur to you.

Step 5: Direct your attention to the present moment and the activities of the day to help you step off the mental merry-go-round until the next worry period. Try to do something positive and pleasant to distract yourself.

Step 6: When the next period arrives, set aside what you're doing and go to the worry place. Reflect on the worries and thoughts you wrote down. Write any thoughts or solutions you have while you worry or dwell for the time you set aside. If the worries or other thoughts you wrote down no longer seem important, go back to what you were doing prior to the worry or dwelling period.

Step 7: After a week or two, drop one of the periods and spread the remaining periods across the day. Continue this until you have just one or two periods for the day.

Now, you try it. Identify a problem or event that you're worrying about or dwelling on and develop a plan to slow the mental merry-go-round.

Use the blank My Slow the Mental Merry-Go-Round Worksheet below or download a blank copy from http://www.newharbinger.com/49197.

My Slow the Mental Merry-Go-Round Worksheet

Instructions: Select several times each day to worry or dwell on events or situations. Then, select how much time you plan to worry or dwell (set goal of at least ten minutes). When the worry or dwelling time arrives, give the worry or dwelling your full attention. When you begin to worry or dwell between the periods you designated, remind yourself that you'll have plenty of uninterrupted time to worry or dwell and then distract yourself or, better yet, practice mindfulness of the breath or engage in a mindful activity. If postponing is working well, then slowly decrease the frequency or length of the worry or dwelling time. Remember, be realistic. The average person worries 5 to 10% of the time. The goal of postponing is to significantly decrease the frequency, intensity, and duration of your worry or dwelling, not eliminate it.

Date: ____________________

	Time of Day (a.m. or p.m.)																		
Week	*6*	*7*	*8*	*9*	*10*	*11*	*12*	*1*	*2*	*3*	*4*	*5*	*6*	*7*	*8*	*9*	*10*	*11*	*12*
1																			
2																			
3																			
4																			
5																			

Comments:

more to do

Describe what it was like to postpone worry or dwelling. Was it easy or difficult?

Did you discover that the worries or thoughts you wrote down sometimes seemed less important when you reflected on them during the worry or dwelling period?

List the kinds of worries you tend to have most often and how they affect you.

List the kinds of events or problems you tend to dwell on and how they affect you.

visualize a calm and positive place 18

for you to know

Your mind is powerful, and one of the most powerful things your mind can do is produce images: calming images that soothe your anxiety and positive images that lift your sadness. Conjuring images is called visualization, and visualizing a calm and positive place can create calm and happy moments throughout your day.

Jada is a good student, but tests make her anxious big time. Often after days of worrying about tests or school projects, she starts to feel down too. Her health education teacher taught her class a cool visualization exercise, and she's started to practice it before tests. On test days, she arrives early and sits on a bench outside the classroom. She then closes her eyes and pictures herself floating on a raft in a calm, warm pool. She imagines the sun warming her skin and hearing sounds of birds chirping in the distance. She feels calm and happy as she welcomes positive feelings that flow over her body like warm water. She visualizes this scene for five minutes. Then she takes a seat in the classroom where she repeats the visualization while the teacher distributes the test booklets. When she opens her eyes, she always feels calmer and more confident about the test.

for you to do

On the lines below, describe the most calm and positive place you can imagine. It could be a real place, like a warm, inviting beach or a soothing, quiet forest you know. Or, it can be a place that exists in your mind.

____

____

____

____

____

____

____

____

Set aside four to five minutes for this visualization activity. (Audio for this visualization is available for download at http://www.newharbinger.com/49197.) Before you start the activity, on a scale from 0 to 10, rate your anxiety level (where 0 is completely relaxed, and 10 is intensely anxious) and sadness level (where 0 is not sad at all and 10 is intensely sad). Write your numbers here:

Anxiety: ____________ Sadness: ____________

Now, find a quiet place to sit comfortably, and close your eyes. Take four slow, deep breaths and then imagine the calm and positive place you just described. As you imagine the scene, look around and notice everything you see. Notice the colors and the textures of the things around you. Feel the peace and calm around you. Listen to any sounds present in this peaceful and positive place. All the sounds are pleasing to you and add to the calm and happiness of the setting. Notice any scents in the air that are also pleasing to you. Inhale the pleasing scents and feel the relaxation calm your entire body and the positive feelings lift your sadness. Notice now that everything you touch feels good to you. The textures against your skin are comforting and calming. As you experience time in this calm and positive place, you're filled with a strong sense of security, serenity, and balance. You feel safe, centered, and grounded.

Sit quietly in this imagined place and feel the peace and calm within you. You will remember this place and this feeling. Then, bring yourself back to the room you're in. As you leave the image, you know that you can take yourself back to this calm and positive place any time that you wish. The calm and positive feelings are always within you.

Now, re-rate your anxiety and sadness level. Write your numbers here:

Anxiety: ______________ Sadness: ______________

Describe how the activity affected your anxiety and sadness. Do you think it helped? Why—or why not?

____

____

____

____

____

Tell why you selected the place in the scene over other places. Why was it calm and positive? Would you change anything about the activity or image?

____

____

____

____

____

more to do

Think through a typical day and identify situations that tend to trigger your anxiety and sadness. Write these situations on the lines below.

____

____

____

____

____

____

____

____

____

____

Now, for the next few days, practice visualizing a calm and positive place in these situations. For example, try the visualization activity while you wait for your turn to give a presentation to the class, or when you remember what a friend said to you that hurt your feelings. The more you practice visualization in these situations, the more confident you'll become that you can quickly change how you feel in those difficult moments everyone has.

relax your body 19

for you to know

Whether you're anxious or sad, your body can feel tense—and a tense body can make your anxiety and sadness worse. This is an easy-to-learn activity that will help relax your body, from your head to your toes. It's super important to do this activity every day, usually just before bed. That way, you start each new day with a relaxed body that prevents your anxiety and sadness from spiraling out of control during the day.

In the following activity, you'll tense and then relax five groups of muscles. All kinds of performers do this to loosen up before a performance. For example, concert violinists repeatedly open and close their hands to relax them before they play. Professional basketball players will often shrug their shoulders or shake their heads before they take a free throw. These simple gestures release pent-up tension, which helps muscles perform optimally. Just like famous musicians and athletes, you too can learn to release unwanted muscle tension so that you're less anxious and stressed during the day.

for you to do

Before you begin, rate your body tension level on a scale from 0 to 10 (where 0 means your body is completely relaxed with no tension at all and 10 means your body is highly tense): ____________

Now, sit or lie down with your arms by your sides, and uncross your legs if they're crossed. Close your eyes. (Audio for this exercise is available for download at http://www.newharbinger.com/49197.)

1. Start by squeezing your eyes tight, scrunch your nose as if you've smelled a rotten egg, pull the edges of your mouth back toward your ears into a forced smile, and bite down to tense your mouth and jaw. Hold this position for the count of fifteen. Then, slowly release your eyes, nose, mouth, and jaw. Relax your face so all the wrinkles disappear, your face is smooth and relaxed, your cheeks feel soft, and your tongue is loose in your mouth. Notice how different this feels from when your face was tight and tense. Your muscles cannot hold a tense, tight position for very long, and it's important for you to learn the difference between tension and relaxation so that you can relax your muscles when you notice they're tense.

2. Now, move to your neck and shoulders. Drop your chin to your chest and pull your shoulders up to your ears. Hold this position for the count of fifteen, observing the tension in your neck and shoulder muscles. Now, release, let your shoulders drop down, and relax your head. Hold this relaxed pose for the count of fifteen.

3. Next, move to your hands and arms. Make fists with your hands and cross your arms at the wrists. Hold your arms up in front of you and push them together as if you're arm-wrestling with yourself. Hold your arms in this position with your fists clenched for the count of fifteen. Then, let your fists uncurl and your arms slowly fall to your sides. Hold this relaxed position for the count of fifteen. Your arms might feel like wet spaghetti. Notice how your arms feel loose and heavy, and how this feeling of relaxation feels much better than when your muscles were tense and tight.

4. Next, suck in your stomach, making your abdomen hard and tight, and clench your buttock muscles together. Hold this position for the count of fifteen. Notice how the tension feels uncomfortable. Then, release and let your stomach go out further and further while you release your buttock muscles. Hold this position for the count of fifteen.

5. Last, stick your legs straight out in front of you and point your feet toward your head while you scrunch your toes into a tight ball. Hold the position for the count of fifteen, then release and relax your feet and legs for the count of fifteen. Your legs might feel loose and floppy, as they relax.

You might notice as you go through all these muscle exercises, tensing and relaxing, that you're starting to feel calmer. You feel grounded as if you're melting into the floor. Your muscles might feel heavy and loose, and your whole body is beginning to feel relaxed. You're in charge of how your body feels, and you're commanding your muscles to relax. You can repeat these five steps to relax your body even more, beginning again with your eyes closed.

Now, rate your body tension level again, as you did when you began the body relaxation activity. Use the same 0 to 10 scale (where 0 means your body is completely relaxed with no tension at all and 10 means your body is highly tense): ____________

more to do

Describe what it was like to tense and relax your body.

____

____

____

____

____

____

Describe what you noticed as your body relaxed.

____

____

____

____

People tend to feel tense in different muscles of their bodies. For some people, it's their neck and shoulders. For others, it's their back. List the muscles that you noticed were most tense during the activity.

Next time you practice this activity, tense and relax these muscles several times before you move to the next muscle group.

Describe how it felt to have a completely relaxed body.

What did you notice about your anxiety and sadness? Did it decrease a little?

release stress instantly 20

for you to know

Sometimes you want stress relief and you want it now. You don't have ten minutes to breathe or twenty minutes to relax your body. You want to feel less tense and more relaxed instantly. This activity combines the muscle relaxation and visualization techniques that you've already learned into a technique that relaxes you in a few seconds.

Devon hates to wait for his teacher to distribute the exams before the test. He hates to wait on the bench for the coach to call him onto the field. He hates to wait for his friend to respond to a text he sent about whether he's invited to a party next week. Devon hates to wait because he knows the longer he waits for these things to happen, the more anxious and stressed he feels. One day, his coach taught the team an instant-stress-release tool. Now, when he's waiting and feeling anxious or stressed or when he's about to do something that he knows tends to stress him out, he uses the instant-stress-release technique. In a couple of seconds, he feels better, like magic.

for you to do

Audio for this exercise is available for download at http://www.newharbinger.com/49197.

Follow these steps to release stress instantly:

1. Grab two tennis balls, one in each hand. If you don't have tennis balls, use balled up washcloths or socks.

2. Close your eyes and squeeze the tennis balls as you imagine squeezing toothpaste out of a tube or juice out of a lemon. Squeeze for five seconds, then release.

3. Squeeze again for five seconds as you imagine squeezing toothpaste out of a tube or juice out of a lemon, then release. Repeat three times.

With practice, you'll bring on the relaxation response in a few seconds just by imagining squeezing the toothpaste or lemon and releasing the tension in your hands.

more to do

Describe what it was like for you to do this activity. Describe the first signs you noticed that your body was relaxing.

____

____

____

____

____

Try this technique when you feel a little sad or down. Describe what you notice. Do you feel a little more energy? Is your mind a little clearer?

___

___

___

Now that you know how to release stress instantly, circle the situations in which you might use the technique:

Waiting for the teacher to hand out tests	Waiting for your coach to send you into the game
Giving a presentation to the class	Taking a driver's test
Going on a first date	Interviewing for a job
Having a difficult conversation with a friend	Disagreeing with your parents or teachers
Getting a break-up text	Trying something new
Waiting to learn how you did on a test	Following an argument with a friend

The list of situations above is short and likely doesn't cover the many situations that can cause you to feel anxious, stressed, or down. Think through a typical week and list the situations in your life in which the instant stress release technique might help:

___

___

___

___

___

21 meditate on gratitude

for you to know

Unlike other meditations, when you meditate on gratitude, you not only relax your body but you also generate feelings of happiness. Spending time with gratitude can decrease your anxiety and sadness. As you regularly meditate on gratitude, you'll notice more to be grateful for and the feeling of comfort and happiness expanding in your life.

Atisha went to her school counselor, Ms. Wilson, for help with her anxiety and sadness. Ms. Wilson suggested Atisha try meditation, but not just any meditation. Ms. Wilson suggested Atisha meditate on gratitude. Atisha didn't feel particularly grateful at the moment. She just broke up with her girlfriend, and she wasn't doing well in her classes. On top of that, her mom told her last week that she and her dad were getting a divorce. Ms. Wilson told Atisha that she knew that things were hard for her right now. She understood that Atisha was skeptical that there was much in her life to feel grateful for, but Ms. Wilson was confident that if she spent a little time with gratitude, she would feel less down and stressed. Atisha liked and trusted Ms. Wilson and agreed to give it a try.

for you to do

You can practice this meditation at the start of your day or at the very end before bedtime. (Audio for this meditation is available for download at http://www.newharbinger.com/49197.) Before you start the activity, rate your anxiety level on a scale from 0 to 10 (where 0 is completely relaxed, and 10 is intensely anxious) and sadness level (where 0 not sad at all and 10 is intensely sad). Write your numbers here:

Anxiety: ______________ Sadness: ______________

Find a quiet place to sit comfortably, and close your eyes. Take in a long, slow, deep breath and then exhale slowly through your lips as if you're blowing a bubble. Take in another long, slow, deep breath and exhale slowly. Feel any tension melt away as you gradually relax. Feel yourself drifting into a state of deep comfort and relaxation.

Continue to breathe slowly and gently as you bring your awareness to the top of your head. Picture a warm, comforting light spreading from the top of your head down to your toes. Feel each muscle relax as the warm, comforting light touches it. Feel your muscles relax as the light washes over you, surrounding and protecting you. Take in two more long deep breaths as you relax fully.

In this safe, relaxed, comfortable state, reflect on all for which you're grateful: loved ones, friends, sunshine through the window, fresh air, the sounds of songbirds. Reflect on whatever might come to mind: the meal you had earlier, the nice compliment from a friend, the movement of your body, the breath in your lungs.

As each thing you're grateful for appears in your mind, picture yourself saying "Thank you" to each. Picture the person you're grateful for standing in front of you as you tell them "Thank you." Picture yourself telling the person how grateful you are for them and why. Try to make the image of the person and the feeling as real as you can. Move through your senses—sight, smell, touch, taste, sound—so that you can taste the delicious cookie or hear the sound of your friend's voice. Say "Thank you" for these wonderful experiences.

Now, allow the feeling of deep gratitude to enter your body. Notice where the feeling of deep gratitude is in your body. Notice any lightness, happiness, peace. This is the feeling of gratitude as it washes away tension, sadness, and anxiety. Spend as much time with the feeling of gratitude as you like.

When you're ready, end the gratitude meditation with the following affirmations:

> *Thank you for the many gifts I receive each day.*

> *Thank you for the many kindnesses and blessings bestowed on me today.*

It's okay if the affirmations feel a little hokey or a little hard to believe at first. Try saying them anyway and being open, as nonjudgmentally as you can, to what arises within you when you say them.

Now, gently move your fingers and toes, open your eyes, and give yourself a few moments to center. Encourage yourself to bring the feelings of gratitude you cultivated in this meditation with you as you go through your day.

Now, re-rate your anxiety and sadness levels. Write your numbers here:

Anxiety: ______________ Sadness: ______________

Describe what it was like for you to spend time with gratitude in this way.

____

____

____

____

Describe how time with gratitude affected your anxiety and sadness and why.

____

____

____

____

more to do

Write why you selected the specific people and things in your gratitude meditation.

Would you change anything about the meditation?

List other affirmations you could add to the end of the gratitude meditation and describe why.

Describe anything you liked or disliked about the gratitude meditation.

22 savor a pleasant moment

for you to know

Savoring means to enjoy a pleasant taste or smell, such as savoring the taste and smell of a warm chocolate chip cookie. You can savor pleasant moments in time too. Savoring pleasant moments is an easy way to lessen your anxiety and to lift the blues.

Binh was feeling stressed and down when she arrived home from school. As she entered the kitchen, she saw her mother sitting at the table in a pool of sunlight. Her eyes were closed and her hands were wrapped around a steaming cup of jasmine tea. Without opening her eyes, her mother whispered, "I'm savoring this moment." Binh snorted and started to pull books from her backpack. Binh's mother opened her eyes and nodded at the chair beside her—"Why don't you slow down and savor this moment with me?" Her mother made a cup of tea for Binh and told her to close her eyes. As Binh savored the sun on her cheek and the fragrance of jasmine rising in a cloud of steam, she felt the stress of the day begin to lighten. As she lingered in the pleasant moment, she felt lighter and a bit happier. When Binh opened her eyes, her mother was looking at her. "There's always time to savor a pleasant moment," she said.

for you to do

Have you savored a pleasant moment like the one Binh had with her mom? Savoring a pleasant moment works best when you try to remember everything about it—where you were and when it happened, who you were with and how you felt. Use the blank My Savor a Pleasant Moment Worksheet below or download a copy from http://www.newharbinger.com/49197.

My Savor a Pleasant Moment Worksheet

Instructions: Follow these steps to create and savor a pleasant moment.

<table>
<tr><td rowspan="2">Step 1:</td><td colspan="2">Before you start the activity, on a scale from 0 to 10, rate your anxiety level (where 0 is completely relaxed, and 10 is intensely anxious) and sadness level (where 0 is not sad at all and 10 is intensely sad).</td></tr>
<tr><td>Anxiety:</td><td>Sadness:</td></tr>
<tr><td>Step 2:</td><td colspan="2">List three good times you had recently (the time you spent doing a favorite activity, a favorite place you've visited, good times you shared with friends or family, a success in life).</td></tr>
<tr><td colspan="3"></td></tr>
<tr><td colspan="3"></td></tr>
<tr><td colspan="3"></td></tr>
</table>

Step 3:	*Pick one of the good times from the list above and picture the moment in your mind. Then, write the elements of the story in the spaces below.*
Describe where you were and what was happening? What did you hear, smell, see?	
Describe the good feelings that you felt (happy, proud, joyful, loved).	
Describe the thoughts going through your mind when you were feeling good feelings.	
Describe your role in making this moment happen. How did you make it happen?	
Imagine this good time leads to more good moments and good feelings in the future. Describe what you imagine could happen then.	
Step 4:	*Now that you've created a story about your good time and good feelings, read through it again. Finally, close your eyes and savor your good time by replaying your story in your mind.*
Step 5:	*Re-rate you anxiety and sadness levels. Write your numbers here.*
	Anxiety: / Sadness:

more to do

Describe how savoring a pleasant moment affected your anxiety and sadness.

____

____

____

Describe anything that you liked about savoring a pleasant moment.

____

____

____

Describe anything that you didn't like about savoring a pleasant moment.

____

____

____

When you're anxious or down, you may have trouble sleeping too. Savoring a pleasant moment can help sleep come more easily. Try the activity tonight while you wait for sleep to come. Then, the next day, describe what that was like for you.

____

____

____

23 recover from mistakes

for you to know

Worrying about making mistakes—whether you're worrying about dropping a pass, forgetting an assignment, or missing a test question—can fill your days with intense anxiety and dread. But no matter how careful or smart you are or how much you study and practice, you're going to make mistakes. When it comes to mistakes, the trick is to know how to bounce back from them rather than try to prevent them at all costs.

Angela is worrying nonstop about missing shots from the free throw line. Usually, Angela sinks them with ease, but during the last big game, she missed one. Since then, no matter how much she practices, she can't get the ball in the hoop. Angela's coach, Ms. Dewitt, noticed and told Angela that it looked like she had a bad case of the "yips"—something that happens to athletes when they become flustered and can't perform under pressure. She said that yips happen when athletes worry too much about making mistakes rather than planning how they'll recover from a mistake if they make one. Ms. Dewitt then taught Angela three steps to recover quickly from a mistake:

Step 1: Use a physical signal to start to recover from a mistake. *Physical signals anchor your mind and body. They're a great way to start mistake recovery, particularly in sports where you're focused on physical effort, but also in other kinds of stressful moments. For example, in tennis, if you feel your serves or shots are starting to miss the mark, you might walk across the back baseline a few feet or twirl the racket twice in your hand. In a test, when you're having some trouble concentrating because you're too anxious or stressed, you might open and close your hands three times, or put your pencil down and pick it up again.*

Step 2: Take several slow, deep breaths. *Take several slow, deep breaths to clear your head and recenter your body. If you're running down the field, just take a deep breath and blow it out forcefully.*

Step 3: Repeat a focus word or phrase. *Use a simple word or phrase to refocus on what's important: the next question on the test or the ball that's in play. If you're focusing on a word or phrase, you can't focus on the mistake. For example, "move on," "next shot," and "next question" are great refocus phrases.*

At the next practice, Angela tried her new mistake recovery plan.

Mistake:	Describe the mistake you're worried about making.
	When I'm taking a shot at the free-throw line.
Step 1:	Describe the physical signal that starts your mistake recovery.
	Bounce the ball three times and nod my head to signal, "Yes, I can."
Step 2:	Describe how you'll breathe.
	Deep breath in and quick breath out. Do this twice.
Step 3:	Describe the focus word or phrase.
	Yes, I can.

for you to do

Think about the kind of mistakes you tend to worry about making. Do you worry that you'll stumble over a word during a presentation to your class? Do you worry that you'll make a bad pass during the next soccer game? Do you panic when you come to a question on a test that you don't know? Or, do you worry that you'll hit a wrong note during your piano recital?

If you worry about making mistakes, develop your own mistake recovery plan. Use the blank My Recover from Mistakes Worksheet or download a copy from http://www.newharbinger.com/49197.

My Recover from Mistakes Worksheet

Instructions: First, describe the mistake you're worried about making. Then, follow the four steps to create a mistake recovery plan.

Mistake:	Describe the mistake you're worried about making.
Step 1:	Describe the physical signal that starts your mistake recovery.
Step 2:	Describe how you'll breathe.
Step 3:	Describe the focus word or phrase.

more to do

Describe what it was like for you the first time you used your mistake recovery plan.

Tell how the mistake recovery plan affected your anxiety level.

Describe other areas in which a mistake recovery plan might help lower your anxiety (public speaking, performances, taking tests, talking to people you don't know).

List other focus words or phrases you might try in step 3 of your mistake recovery plan.

24 consider the pluses and minuses

for you to know

There are pluses and minuses to what you do and what you think. The biggest minus is acting and thinking in ways that keep you trapped in a lot of anxiety and depression. Considering the pluses and minuses can help you decide whether you want to continue to act and think in unhelpful ways or to change them.

Aniya has felt very depressed for the last few months and has stopped hanging out with her friends. She thinks that, because she's so depressed, she'll spoil everyone's fun. She makes one excuse after another. She tells her friends that she has to babysit her brother, or that she has too much homework, or that her mom won't let her go. Now every weekend, she's alone in her bedroom thinking about the fun her friends are having and feeling more and more depressed.

One day at the dinner table, Aniya watched her brother list the pluses and minuses of each college on his college application list. He said it helped him think through his options. Aniya decided to apply pluses and minuses to her situation and the belief that she would spoil her friends' fun because she's depressed.

Write down what you're thinking or considering doing:
I don't want to hang out with my friends because I think I'll spoil their fun because I'm depressed.
List all the pluses for what you're thinking or considering doing:
If I don't hang out with my friends, then I don't have to explain to them why they haven't seen me. If I don't hang out with my friends, then I don't take the chance that I'll spoil their fun. If I don't hang out with my friends, then they won't know I'm depressed, and I don't have to feel embarrassed.

List all the minuses for what you're thinking or considering doing:
If I keep avoiding my friends, I'll never know whether I'll spoil their fun or not.
I feel lonely sitting in my bedroom when my friends are having fun.
Hanging out with my friends is about the only fun thing I do.
I feel like a bad friend because I don't hang out with them.
I feel guilty when I make up an excuse for why I can't hang out with them.
It's possible I might feel better if I took a chance and hung out with my friends.
Add the total pluses and the total minuses and write below:
Pluses: 3 Minuses: 6
If there are more minuses than pluses for what you're thinking or considering doing, how could you think or act differently that would result in more pluses?
I'm going to hang out one time with my friends and see if I spoil their fun. I don't have to stay the entire time. I can tell them I'm not feeling well if I start to feel more depressed, but probably once I'm with them I'll feel a little better.

for you to do

Now, you try it. Use the blank My Consider the Pluses and Minuses Worksheet below or download a copy from http://www.newharbinger.com/49197.

My Consider the Pluses and Minuses Worksheet

Instructions: First, write down what you're thinking or considering doing. Then, follow the following steps to consider the pluses and minuses of a thought or action.

Write down what you're thinking or considering doing:
List all the pluses for what you're thinking or considering doing:
List all the minuses for what you're thinking or considering doing:
Add the total pluses and the total minuses and write below:
Pluses: ______________ Minuses: ______________
If there are more minuses than pluses for what you're thinking or considering doing, how could you think or act differently that would result in more pluses?

What did you learn from considering the pluses and minuses?

____

____

____

____

____

How did you feel after you completed the pluses and minuses exercise?

____

____

____

more to do

What are the kinds of thoughts that make you anxious or sad? How might considering the pluses and minuses of believing the thought help you feel better?

___

___

___

___

Considering pluses and minuses helps with almost every decision. You can use it to decide small things, like what to wear to a party or whom to invite to the dance. You can use it for big decisions too, like which colleges to apply to or what kind of job to take. List several decisions you're struggling to make right now.

___

___

___

___

When you're feeling stuck, considering pluses and minuses can help you decide what to do to get unstuck. List several ways you're feeling stuck right now.

___

___

___

___

___

solve problems 25

for you to know

When you're anxious or depressed, even little problems can feel huge. That's because when you're anxious or depressed, you feel overwhelmed or hopeless, or both. But the reality is that you can learn to solve many of the problems you face quickly. Knowing that you can solve most problems that life throws your way will help you feel calm, capable, and hopeful.

Mehera often feels overwhelmed by life. There's too much homework. A friend won't return her texts. Her parents ask her to babysit her kid sister. One problem after another comes at her until she's paralyzed with anxiety and hopelessness. One day, Ms. Gaspari, Mehera's health education teacher, noticed that Mehera seemed distracted and asked her what was going on. Through tears, Mehera listed all the things that she was dealing with: homework, friends, babysitting. Ms. Gaspari smiled and asked Mehera what ideas she had to solve these problems. When Mehera shrugged, Ms. Gaspari said that solving problems was just a matter of applying six steps, which she then wrote on the board. Ms. Gaspari suggested they apply the six steps to the problem of too much homework, which was overwhelming Mehera and causing her to have trouble getting some homework assignments to her teachers on time.

Step 1: Identify the problem.

Ms. Gaspari started by saying, "A problem well put is half solved," and explained that the first step in solving a problem is to be really clear about what it is you want to change. Ms. Gaspari asked Mehera why she thought that she had too much homework. Mehera paused. She had never thought about why she had too much homework. To her, it was just a fact. As she thought about it, however, she said that perhaps it was because she was taking two AP classes and had recently volunteered to tutor several younger kids in math because it would look good on her college applications. Ms. Gaspari said it sounded as if the problem was that Mehera had two AP classes and a volunteer job, and this meant that she had a lot more homework than usual and less time to do it. As Mehera nodded, Ms. Gaspari wrote the problem on the board: "More homework and less time to do it."

Step 2: Brainstorm solutions that might help.

Ms. Gaspari then said the next step was the fun part of solving problems. "This is when you can get creative," she said, and encouraged Mehera to think of as many solutions to the problem as she could, no matter how crazy, silly, or impossible the solution might seem. Ms. Gaspari knew that anxiety and depression can shut down your ability to brainstorm, so she encouraged Mehera to practice thinking outside the box. Mehera and Ms. Gaspari came up with the following solutions. Several of them were kind of silly:

Drop one of the AP classes. Drop the tutoring job. Meet with one of the peer tutors to help get through the homework faster. Ask if I can switch to an AP history teacher who doesn't assign as much homework. Drop out of school so I never have to do homework again. Pay my older brother to do my homework.

Step 3: Consider the costs and benefits of each solution.

Next, Mehera and Ms. Gaspari considered the costs and benefits of each solution, to help them decide which solution would be best for Mehera to try.

Solution 1: Drop one of the AP classes.	
Costs	*Benefits*
My college application won't look as good. My parents might be upset with me. I will miss my friends in the class.	Dropping an AP class gives me quick relief.

<table>
<tr><td colspan="2">Solution 2: Drop the tutoring job.</td></tr>
<tr><th>Costs</th><th>Benefits</th></tr>
<tr><td>My college application won't look as good.

My math teacher, who helped me get the tutoring job, might be disappointed.</td><td>My parents might be okay with this.

I'll still see my friends.

It will free up at least three hours per week.

Dropping the tutoring job doesn't look as bad on my college application as dropping an AP class.</td></tr>
<tr><td colspan="2">Solution 3: Meet with one of the peer tutors to help get through the homework faster.</td></tr>
<tr><th>Costs</th><th>Benefits</th></tr>
<tr><td>This takes time away from homework.

I don't like any of the peer tutors.</td><td>Peer tutors might have some ideas on speeding things up.

Doesn't affect how I look on my college application.</td></tr>
<tr><td colspan="2">Solution 4: Ask if I can switch to an AP history teacher who doesn't assign as much homework.</td></tr>
<tr><th>Costs</th><th>Benefits</th></tr>
<tr><td>This might upset my current AP history teacher.

Some of the other students might get upset if the school allows me to do this.

I'll miss my friends in the current AP class.</td><td>If the other history class is easier, that might reduce my homework load.</td></tr>
</table>

Solution 5: Drop out of school so I never have to do homework again.	
Costs	**Benefits**
No school. No future. My parents will freak out. I'll miss my friends. I'll die of shame and guilt.	No homework ever again.
Solution 6: Ask my older brother to do my homework.	
Costs	**Benefits**
He'll say no, so what's the point? He might tell my parents, and then I'm grounded for life. My parents will freak out.	I don't have to do my homework (but I might have to do his).
Step 4: Select and apply a solution.	

Mehera and Ms. Gaspari reviewed the list of possible solutions and decided to try "Drop the tutoring job." It was the easiest solution to do and likely wouldn't make things worse for Mehera in a big way. Ms. Gaspari then helped Mehera think through when she would drop the tutoring job, whom to talk to about this, and the best way to say this. Mehera agreed to give herself two weeks after she dropped the tutoring job to see if this extra time helped her to complete her homework on time.

Step 5: Evaluate how well the solution worked.

Mehera dropped the tutoring job, but after two weeks, she was still overwhelmed and stressed.

Step 6: Decide the next step.

Mehera decided to try another of the solutions. She'd meet with one of the peer tutors a couple of times to see if they had some ideas to cut down on the time it takes to complete her homework. When she met with one of the tutors, he suggested that she skip the optional problems her history teacher assigned. He said he did that, and he still did well in the history class. This helped immediately, and Mehera did well on the next history pop quiz.

Mehera applied the six steps to other problems that came up for her. It even worked for friend problems. As she learned to solve problems, she felt less anxious and down about her life.

for you to do

Now, describe a problem that you're facing and go through the six steps. Use the blank My Solve Problems Worksheet below or download a copy from http://www.newharbinger.com/49197.

My Solve Problems Worksheet

Instructions: First, identify the problem. Next, brainstorm at least five possible solutions. When brainstorming, don't rule out a possible solution. Give yourself permission to generate as many possible solutions that you can think of no matter how silly or impractical they are. Then, select one of the solutions and try it. The best solution is the one most likely to work and least likely to cause you more problems. There is seldom a perfect solution to a problem, but there are many good solutions that can help a little while not making things worse. You can't know whether a solution works until you try it. The final step in the problem-solving program is to take a look at how well the solution worked. To help you decide how well a solution worked, imagine a target. If you hit the bullseye, your solution worked great. This means you got what you wanted *and* it didn't create other problems for you. If the solution hit the target but wasn't a bullseye, this means you'll want to modify the solution a little. If the solution missed the target completely, this means it didn't work at all or worse yet, created more problems for you. Select another solution from the list or brainstorm more. Sometimes, trying one solution leads you to other solutions you didn't think of the first time you brainstormed.

Step 1: Identify the problem.	
Step 2: Brainstorm solutions that might help.	
Step 3: Consider the costs and benefits of each solution.	
Solution 1:	
Costs	*Benefits*
Solution 2:	
Costs	*Benefits*

Solution 3:	
Costs	*Benefits*
Solution 4:	
Costs	*Benefits*
Step 4: Select and apply a solution.	
Step 5: Evaluate how well the solution worked.	
Step 6: Decide the next step.	

more to do

List the typical problems that you face at home and school or with friends and family. Place a ✓ by the problems that tend to arise repeatedly in your life.

Describe why you think these problems arise so often for you and how they make you feel (anxious, depressed, angry, guilty).

Choose one of the problems that tend to arise repeatedly for you and apply the six steps to solve this problem. Describe what happened and how you felt before and after the process.

26 break things down

for you to know

When you're anxious or depressed, it's harder to get things done. You convince yourself that you'll do it later when you have more energy or feel less stressed. As you put things off, your anxiety builds, your mood crashes, and you feel more and more overwhelmed. Now it feels impossible to start a project, even a small one, much less finish it. To get things moving, it helps to break a big project into smaller projects or steps.

Aleah was having trouble getting started on writing a three-paragraph essay. She was feeling anxious and depressed about school, about her social life, and about the load of homework ahead of her that night. No matter how hard she tried to concentrate on the essay, she instantly felt overwhelmed and put off working on it.

Then Aleah's older sister, Aafreen, popped her head into the bedroom. She could see that Aleah was upset and asked if she could help. Aleah told her sister that she was having trouble starting the essay. Aafreen smiled and suggested that she break the essay down into steps. "That's what I do, and it helps me get going." They then broke the essay project into small steps and wrote them down:

Read the instructions for the essay.

Skim the chapter that has to do with the essay.

List the topic sentences for each paragraph.

Write the first paragraph.

Write the second paragraph.

Write the third paragraph.

Ask Aafreen to proof it.

Include her suggestions.

Spell-check the essay.

Print the essay.

As Aleah started to break the project down, she began to relax a little as she realized that she would have time to finish the essay and her other homework that night.

for you to do

Follow these steps to break things down:

Step 1: Think of a project that you're putting off. It could be a school project, home project, or anything else.

Step 2: Ask yourself, "How many parts can I divide this task into?" Then, divide the task or project into as many small steps as you can think of.

Step 3: Look at each step. Rate how confident (0 to 10, where 10 is extremely confident) you are that you could start and complete the step as you described it. Try for a confidence level of 8 or greater. If you feel less than 8, break that small step into a couple of smaller steps.

Step 4: Keep breaking down each step until you have steps that you're very confident (8 or greater) that you can start and complete.

Now, you try it. Use the blank My Break Things Down Worksheet below or download a copy from http://www.newharbinger.com/49197.

My Break Things Down Worksheet

Instructions: Think of a project or task that you're having trouble starting. Now, break this project down into small steps. For each step, estimate how confident (0 to 10) you are that you can start and complete the step. Keep breaking the project into steps until you're very confident (8 or greater) that you can start and complete each step.

Project or task:	
Step	*Confidence Level (0-10)*

Describe what it was like to break a project into small steps. As you felt more confident, did you begin to feel less overwhelmed? Did the project start to feel more doable?

____

____

____

more to do

List several projects or tasks that are coming up that you could break down.

27 manage time

for you to know

When you're chronically behind schedule, you're likely feeling chronically anxious or down too. When you can't manage time, you get less done, and often what you do get done is done at the last minute. This is a formula to make you anxious: you worry you won't get the work done, or when you do get it done, you're exhausted and often disappointed with what you turned out at the last minute. This only brings you down.

Juan is always running late for things, and he has a lot of things to do: classes, student council, soccer practices and games, homework, and mass on Sundays. He has jobs around the house too: cleaning his room, washing the car, taking out the recycling, and helping his mom grocery shop on Saturday. Juan's schedule is so packed that he often has to work very late to get all his homework done. Also, Juan is at least five minutes late to almost everything. One day, he asks his friend Simone how she manages her time. Simone is as busy as Juan is but is always on top of things. Simone tells Juan that her piano teacher taught her four Rs to help her find more time to practice. Simone taught the four Rs of time management to Juan too:

> **Record**: *You might already use a scheduling tool, such as an electronic calendar or a paper day timer, planner, or an assignment book. Regardless of the scheduling tool, the most important first step in managing time is to schedule it. Decide on a particular day to make your schedule for the week. For example, Sunday nights work best because you haven't officially started the week. It can help to link scheduling your time with an activity you already do, such as putting away your clean clothes or filling your pill organizer box, if you do these things on a particular day. Complete your schedule for all seven days of the week. If you think you may have a commitment but you're not sure, place a question mark for that activity to hold the time, just in case. And most important—always check your schedule before you make a plan, and when you make a plan, record it in the schedule immediately.*

Remind: *Create reminders so you remember to create your schedule for the week and then so you remember to check your schedule several times each day. Set a timer on your phone or laptop, place a sticky note on your desk, or ask a friend to text you a few hours before something super important.*

Review: *Every morning when you first get up, review your schedule for the day. Also, review your schedule before lunch and on the way home to make sure that you don't forget a commitment. When someone asks you to do something or before you make a plan, review your schedule before you say yes. It only takes a second, and it's easier to say no when you're asked than it is to say no later when you realize that you're double-booked.*

Reward: *Reward yourself each day and at the end of the week when you've followed the first three Rs. You can even schedule the reward. For example, you might schedule some extra time to play your favorite video game or time to give yourself a mani-pedi. You might schedule a little reward just after you create the schedule for the upcoming week to help you continue to manage your time in this way.*

for you to do

Now, you try it. Use the blank My Daily Schedule Worksheet below or download a copy from http://www.newharbinger.com/49197. Make seven copies of the worksheet and then, for each day of the next week, follow the four Rs to manage your time.

My Daily Schedule Worksheet

Instructions: Each day, schedule the day by writing what you'll do each hour of the day. Try to be as specific as you can. For example, write, "work on English essay" rather than "do homework."

Day:	Date:
05:00 a.m.	
06:00 a.m.	
07:00 a.m.	
08:00 a.m.	
09:00 a.m.	
10:00 a.m.	
11:00 a.m.	
12:00 noon	
01:00 p.m.	
02:00 p.m.	
03:00 p.m.	
04:00 p.m.	
05:00 p.m.	
06:00 p.m.	
07:00 p.m.	
08:00 p.m.	
09:00 p.m.	
10:00 p.m.	
11:00 p.m.	
12:00 midnight	

more to do

Describe what it was like to use the four Rs of time management. How did it affect your anxiety and depression? Was it easy or difficult to do?

Which of the four Rs do you need the most help with and why?

28 communicate clearly

for you to know

Whether you're anxious or depressed, learning to communicate clearly with people is an important skill. Communicating clearly strengthens relationships so that you're less prone to feel lonely and depressed. Communicating clearly also helps you avoid arguments that can fuel your anxiety and stress, or helps you feel less anxious about meeting new people and building new friendships. You can improve your ability to communicate clearly by learning a few simple skills.

Dana often worries that he's not a good communicator. He thinks he'll say the wrong thing and people will get angry with him, or they'll think he's rude or a know-it-all. Because he's worried about upsetting people, he doesn't say hello to people at school and has started to avoid returning texts from his friends. Dana is feeling down and lonely, and is now worried that he'll lose the only friends he has.

One day, Mr. George, his health education teacher, saw Dana sitting alone in the cafeteria and sat down next to him. Mr. George asked Dana why he didn't sit with other people at lunch. Dana told Mr. George, "I'm not a good communicator like the other kids are. That's why they don't want to hang out with me." Mr. George nodded and told Dana that communication was a skill, and, like any skill, he could learn to communicate clearly with a little practice. He suggested that Dana start by learning to send the kind of messages he wants to send.

for you to do

Communication is about sending messages, and clear communication is about sending messages that people understand and are open to receive. Often, people send you-messages, and you-messages can make communicating with someone more difficult, particularly when you use words like *never, should,* or *always.* You-messages can put people on the defensive. When you say to a friend, "You never listen to me," it sounds as if you're attacking her. When you send you-messages, people stop listening and sometimes get upset.

I-messages, on the other hand, help you to clearly and honestly express yourself. An I-message tends to put people at ease because it sounds as if it's about you and not about them, even when sometimes it is about them. Using I-messages rather than you-messages improves your relationships with friends, family, and teachers, and stronger relationships mean less worry that you'll lose friends or upset people. An I-message includes three parts: **I feel...when you...because....**

Situation	You-message	I-message
You're anxious because Jessica sits with Dara at lunch and doesn't invite you to join them.	"You ***never*** sit and talk with me at lunch anymore."	"**I feel** hurt **when you** sit with Dara at lunch and don't invite me to join **because** it makes me think that you don't want to be my friend anymore."
You're sad because your friend Alonso picked Asa for his team and didn't pick you.	"You ***should*** pick me because I'm your best friend, not Asa."	"**I feel** upset **when you** pick Asa without asking me **because** it makes me think that I'm not your best friend anymore."
You're upset because your mom asked you to clean your room while you're talking to a friend on the phone.	"You ***always*** interrupt me when I'm talking with my friends."	"**I feel** frustrated **when you** ask me to do something when I'm talking to friends **because** it makes me think that you don't care whether I have friends or not."

Think of a situation and then write a you-message and an I-message for the situation. Practice both messages in front of the mirror in private.

____

____

____

____

____

____

Describe how each kind of message makes you feel when you say it to yourself.

____

____

____

____

____

____

____

____

more to do

Clear communication involves more than what you say. It involves how you sound and look when you say it. To communicate clearly, it's important that your body and voice match the message your words are sending. Follow the four Cs of clear communication to ensure that people receive the communication signals you want them to receive.

	What Not to Do	What to Do
Calm voice	Mumble. Shout or yell.	Speak calmly and at a volume suitable to the environment.
Calm body	Clench your fists or point at the person. Slouch. Turn away from the person.	Try a half-smile. Stand tall. Face the person.
Connect with your eyes	Look down or away. Squint.	Maintain eye contact. Open your eyes and raise your eyebrows slightly.
Create space	Get in the person's face. Lean in too close to the person.	Keep an arm's length between you and the other person. Lean back a little.

Now, practice the four Cs in front of a mirror in private. First, try "what not to do," and then try "what to do." Describe how you feel when you talk to yourself in the different ways.

Think about conversations in the past that didn't go the way you wanted them to go. Describe how the wrong four Cs may have contributed to the problem and how the right four Cs could have helped.

stand up for yourself 29

for you to know

When you're anxious or depressed, it can be difficult to stand up for yourself. You might worry that if you say no to people, they won't like you. You might feel too guilty or depressed to tell people who tease or bully you to stop it. Either way, learning to stand up for yourself will help you feel less powerless, less anxious, and better about yourself.

Zion's plate is very full this week. He has a big chemistry exam to study for, and he wants to spend more time preparing for the debate in history class. Also, it's his mom's birthday, and he and his sisters want to give her a big party. Zion was already feeling overwhelmed by the number of things on his plate, and then Ms. Chan, his favorite teacher, asked whether he would be willing to tutor a couple of her students in math this week. Zion thought, "I can't say no to Ms. Chan. She's done so much for me." Zion knows that saying no is the right thing to do, but he doesn't know how to say it. Then he remembered the assertiveness exercise Mr. Bennett had taught in his communication arts class. Mr. Bennett had said that standing up for yourself was sometimes hard, but it was easier when you followed four steps: state the problem, state how it makes you feel, say no or request a change, and get the buy-in.

for you to do

There are many reasons to stand up for yourself, but whether it's saying no, stop, or that it's not your thing, you just follow four steps:

Step 1: State the problem. It is important to describe the facts: for example, "I have to study for my history exam, prepare for my English presentation tomorrow, and you want me to help you with your math homework," or, "Although you say that you're just kidding, you keep teasing me about my new jeans."

Step 2: State how the problem makes you feel. For example, "I feel overwhelmed by the number of things I have to do," or, "I feel hurt because you're my best friend and what you think is important to me."

Step 3: Say no, or request a change. For example, "Although I'd like to help, I can't help you today, but I could help you next time," or, "Please stop teasing me about my jeans."

Step 4: Get the buy-in. For example, "Would that work for you?" or, "Would you do that for me?" The buy-in is important. It makes the other person have to say no to you. This final step puts you in a position of power rather than powerlessness.

Now, you try it. Use the blank My Stand Up For Myself Worksheet below or download a copy from http://www.newharbinger.com/49197.

My Stand Up For Myself Worksheet

Instructions: First, describe the situation in which you want to stand up for yourself. Next, write your responses in each step. In the ***Put it all together*** section, put all the steps together to create a stand up for myself response. Last, practice the response in front of the mirror until you feel confident.

Situation in which you want to stand up for yourself:
Step 1: State the facts of the problem:
Step 2: State how the problem makes you feel:
Step 3: Say no, or request a change:

Step 4: Get the buy-in:
Put it all together:

Describe a situation when it makes sense for you to stand up for yourself.

____

____

Write what you'll say for each of the four steps.

____

____

____

____

Now, practice what you wrote while you stand in front of a mirror until you feel calm and confident.

more to do

There are many situations in which standing up for yourself could help you feel less anxious or depressed. Circle any of the following situations in which you have trouble saying no or standing up for yourself in other ways:

Friends push you to skip class.	Parents ask you to do something when you're in the middle of something else.
Friends ask you to do their homework.	Teachers ask you to do extra work without a good reason.
Friends push you to take sides.	Coaches push you to stay late at practice when you have a lot of homework to do.
Friends push you to do drugs.	Friends tease you.
Parents accuse you of something that you didn't do.	Friends ghost you on social media.

Who do you know who's good at standing up for themselves? What could you learn from these people? Do they follow the four steps?

____

____

____

____

____

____

30 manage conflict and disagreements

for you to know

People who have trouble managing conflict and disagreements tend to feel more anxious or depressed. Their relationships are stressful, less rewarding, and don't last. Conflict and disagreements are a fact of life, but when you know how to manage conflict, your relationships will be stronger, easier, and more fulfilling.

People at school call Kiara and Sarafina "the twins." That's because they have a lot in common. They're the youngest in their families. Their favorite flavor of ice cream is Rocky Road. Their favorite color is purple. They're in nearly all the same classes. They spend a lot of time together and, most of the time, they get along great, but sometimes when they're together, they argue.

After science class one day, they started to argue. Mr. Jeffers asked them to stay behind and chat with him. Mr. Jeffers started by saying, "Remember when I taught you about atomic particles last month. Atomic particles with opposite charges attract and particles with the same charge fly apart. You two are like atomic particles with the same charge. You're so much alike that you're bound to clash." Mr. Jeffers then wrote on the board five Cs to manage conflict and disagreements:

Calm manner. *It's impossible to work through disagreements if you're not calm. Take three or four deep, calming breaths. Ask the other person to meet with you at a later time when you're both calm and relaxed to discuss the problem.*

Clear communication. *Use I-messages rather than you-messages. Say, "I'm upset that you didn't return my text like I asked," rather than, "You didn't return my text like I asked."*

Current problem. *Focus on the current problem and not on past problems. Say "You didn't return my text today," rather than, "You never return my texts quickly," or, "You didn't return my text again."*

Compromise. *Think in terms of getting to a mutually satisfactory understanding. Remember that it's better to be effective than it is to be right. It's not about winning or losing. It's about managing the conflict in order to protect your relationships. For example, if you're arguing with a friend about whether to leave at 7:00 p.m. or 8:00 p.m., compromise and propose that you leave at 7:30 p.m.; or if you're arguing with your mom about whether to do your chores now or later that day, compromise and propose that you do a few chores now and finish the others later.*

Careful words. *Don't call the other person names, such as "idiot," "loser," "jerk," or "stupid." Not only will these words upset the other person, they'll inflame your frustration.*

Kiara and Sarafina agree to practice the five Cs for a couple of weeks. At first, it felt a little fake, but at the end of the first week, they noticed that they were arguing less and that their conflicts ended more quickly. After several more weeks, they were feeling better about themselves and each other. They also noticed that their relationships with their friends and their brothers and sisters were improving too.

for you to do

During disagreements, your emotions can hit fast and hard, and before you know it, you're arguing with the other person. That's why it helps to plan ahead. Hassle plans are a great way to plan for the typical disagreements, conflicts, and other hassles that often arise in your life. Hassle plans include typical situations and the five Cs you just learned:

Hassle:	Dana and I agree to do something, and he's often at least ten minutes late. Most of the time it's no big deal, but sometimes, like when we're going to a movie, it is a big deal. I don't want to miss the beginning of the show.
Calm Manner:	I'll take a couple of slow breaths while I'm waiting for him. I'll ask him if we can talk later, when I'm not in a rush to get to the event or movie. I'll feel more relaxed later and maybe in a little better mood.
Clear Communication:	I'll use I-messages. I'll say, "Dana, I feel really frustrated when we agree to do something and you're late."
Current Problem:	I'll remember to discuss the current problem and not say things like "you always" or "you never," or "you did it again." This just takes us off track and makes Dana defensive.
Compromise:	This isn't about winning or losing the argument. It's about finding a way that Dana and I can have a good time hanging out that works for both of us. Maybe he'll agree to text me if he's running late and tell me when he thinks he'll arrive.
Careful Words:	I won't call Dana "a flake" like I did last time. He's not a flake. In fact, he's late because he tends to try to do too much.

Now, you try it. Use the blank My Hassle Plan Worksheet below or download a copy from http://www.newharbinger.com/49197. Make a copy for every hassle that comes up for you regularly.

My Hassle Plan Worksheet

Instructions: Describe the hassle clearly and how it usually comes up in your life. Next, write what you want to remember for each of the five Cs. The Cs may differ a little based on the type of hassle and with whom you're having a disagreement.

Hassle:	
Calm Manner:	
Clear Communication:	
Current Problem:	
Compromise:	
Careful Words:	

Look back over the hassle plans you created. Practice each one several times in front of a mirror. It's always better to practice what you're going to say (and not say) ahead of time.

more to do

Describe what it was like for you to practice your hassle plan. Would you make any changes to the plan?

Think about your part in disagreements. Which of the five Cs is the most difficult for you to follow and why? Which of the Cs come easier to you and why?

Describe how conflict affects your anxiety and depression.

replace hopelessness with hope 31

for you to know

When people feel anxious or depressed, they view the future as bleak and hopeless. When they feel less anxious or depressed, they view the future as easier and more hopeful. You can learn to replace hopelessness with hope in those moments when you're anxious or sad.

Esperanza is in art class. She loves art and usually this is her best class of the day, but today she's feeling anxious and depressed. Ms. Averson notices that Esperanza isn't her usual self and asks how she's doing. Esperanza tells Ms. Averson that she's stressed about her grades: "I know that I'm not a great student, but I've tried everything to improve my grades. There's no way I'm going to get into college if I don't do better in my classes. I'm feeling pretty hopeless. I don't know what to do."

Ms. Averson nods and tells Esperanza that she understands that school is difficult for her, but she's confident that she'll find a way to improve her grades. "You just need a little dose of hope right now." Ms. Averson then hands Esperanza a shoe box and a basket filled with colored paper, glitter, and markers. "Years ago, my high school art teacher showed me how to make a hope box. It's fun and it's a great way to replace hopelessness with hope. Do you want to try it?"

for you to do

A hope box is a container you fill with items that help you feel inspired, optimistic, and hopeful about the future. You can fill your hope box with anything: pictures, poetry, letters, prayer cards, Bible verses, even mementos, such as a beautiful stone or pressed flower that reminds you of better times. Circle all the categories of items that inspire you and help you feel more optimistic and hopeful. Feel free to add other items that aren't on the list:

Short inspirational newspaper or magazine articles	Inspirational poems or quotes	Photos of friends and special family members
Pictures from magazines	Soothing items like hand lotion, yarn, or cloth to rub	Soothing fragrances like scented candles or lotions
Special items from nature	Small gifts from friends or family members	Reminders to listen to inspirational songs
Award ribbons or medals that you've received	Baby photos of you or of a loved one	A list of events (your prom, wedding, graduation) that you're looking forward to
A favorite scarf or small item of clothing that you like	Programs from fun concerts or sporting events you've attended	Comforting or inspiring letters from friends or family members

Now, decorate the box and place the items in it. Later, if you think of other items, add those to your hope box too. You might ask a trusted friend or family member for ideas. Remember, any item that inspires hope and optimism is great for a hope box.

List the contents of your hope box:

____

____

____

____

____

____

____

____

Identify several items in the hope box and describe why you selected them to inspire hope and optimism:

____

____

____

____

____

____

more to do

Now, pick several times during the day to go through your hope box. Pick up each item and connect with the hopeful feelings it generates for you. If it's a poem or an article, read it aloud to yourself. If it's a special stone or award, hold the item and remember where you were when you found it or when it was given to you. If it's a list of special songs, listen to the songs and sing along.

My Replace Hopelessness with Hope Log

Instructions: Record the day and time of day you spend time with your hope box. Then, circle the number that corresponds to the level (where 1 is low and 5 is high) of anxiety or depression you feel ***before*** and then ***after*** you use the hope box.

Week of:		Anxiety or Depression									
Day	*Time*	*Before Hope Box*					*After Hope Box*				
		1	2	3	4	5	1	2	3	4	5
		1	2	3	4	5	1	2	3	4	5
		1	2	3	4	5	1	2	3	4	5
		1	2	3	4	5	1	2	3	4	5
		1	2	3	4	5	1	2	3	4	5
		1	2	3	4	5	1	2	3	4	5
		1	2	3	4	5	1	2	3	4	5

Describe your experience using the hope box. Which items generated the most hope and optimism? Which items soothed and comforted you the most?

Telling a trusted friend or family member about your hope box can encourage their support during difficult times. They can remind you to go through the hope box or, better yet, go through the hope box with you. Write the names of trusted friends or family members with whom you'd like to share your hope box:

32 get going

for you to know

When you feel depressed, you might start to do less. You might lose your desire to do activities that were once interesting or fun. However, when you stop doing things that are fun or interesting, this only increases your depression. A powerful way to decrease your depressed feelings is to get going and stay involved in your life.

Valentina has been anxious all her life. She mostly worries whether her friends like her, and she's super anxious when meeting new people or giving presentations to the class. Although she has friends, they're friends from kindergarten, and she avoids speaking to new kids at school and doesn't go to parties. Over the last year, her friends have started to invite her less often to go to concerts and parties with them. Now Valentina is depressed and lies on the sofa binge-watching shows, ignoring texts from friends, and sleeping many hours a day.

One day, her mom asks Valentina to watch their favorite show together. Valentina tells her mom that she's too tired and says, "I won't enjoy it anyway." Valentina's mom then sits down to talk to her. She says that she knows Valentina is feeling down but wonders if doing so little is helping her feel better. Valentina says, "No, but nothing I do is any fun, and I feel too tired to try." Valentina's mom explains that when we're feeling down, we have to act first to feel better: "As we get going, we feel less tired." In fact, she adds, once we start doing things, even if they're not fun at first, the fun starts to come back if we keep doing them. Valentina and her mom work out a plan to get Valentina going. After a week, Valentina starts to feel better and to her surprise, her energy comes back, and so does the fun.

for you to do

Circle all the fun activities that you once enjoyed doing, even if just a little, or the activities that you felt proud of when you finished them. Feel free to add your own special fun or proud activities to the list. If you're having trouble coming up with fun things, ask a friend for ideas about the fun things you used to do together.

Dance in your room	Play basketball	Play cards
Text or email a friend	Walk the dog	Plant a flower
Write fan fiction	Watch funny videos	Give a hug
Ride bike or skateboard	Listen to music	Eat lunch with friend
Draw or paint	Organize your clothes or shoes	Sing in your room
Have a friend over	Watch a favorite sport	Bake something
Organize your backpack	Create a new music playlist	Take a warm bath

more to do

Now, create a plan to get going and then track how well it's working for you. Use the blank My Get Going Log below or download a copy from http://www.newharbinger.com/49197. Begin by listing activities that are fun and enjoyable, such as watching a movie or talking to a friend, and activities that you may not enjoy but feel proud of yourself for doing when you complete them, such as organizing your closet or jogging for thirty minutes. Place an X in the day column every time you do the fun or "proud" activity. At the bottom of the form, total the activities you completed each day and your average mood (0 to 10, where 10 is very anxious or very down) for each day. Look at Valentina's fun and proud activities log to see how she did it.

Date: **April 16th**	*Day of Week*						
Fun or Proud Activity	*Su*	*Mo*	*Tu*	*We*	*Th*	*Fr*	*Sa*
Walk Bobbo with Mom.	X		X			X	X
Dance in my room for ten minutes.	X	X		X	X	X	
Text a friend to say hello.		X	X	X		X	
Watch a funny movie with the family.						X	X
Play catch with Bobbo for ten minutes.		X	X		X	X	
Cook dinner with Mom.	X					X	X
Listen to my favorite playlist.	X	X	X		X	X	X
Do arts and crafts project with my sister.	X						X
Total Number of Activities:	5	4	4	2	3	7	5
Average Mood (0–10):	4	5	5	7	7	3	4

My Get Going Log

Instructions: List activities that are fun and enjoyable, such as watching a movie or talking to a friend, and activities that you may not enjoy but feel proud of yourself for doing when you complete, such as organizing your closet or jogging for 30 minutes. Place an **X** in the day column every time you do the fun or proud activity. At the bottom of the form, total the activities you completed each day and your average mood (0-10, where 10 is very anxious or very down) for each day.

Date:	*Day of Week*						
Fun or Proud Activity	*Su*	*Mo*	*Tu*	*We*	*Th*	*Fr*	*Sa*
Total Number of Activities:							
Average Mood (0-10):							

Describe what it was like to try fun or proud activities, even though you didn't feel like doing them.

face uncomfortable feelings 33

for you to know

It's natural for people who feel intensely anxious and depressed to avoid these uncomfortable feelings. However, avoiding these uncomfortable feelings is the primary reason people stay anxious and depressed. Although it's counterintuitive, facing rather than avoiding your anxious and depressed feelings is the best way to feel less anxious and depressed over time.

Neal and Nell both avoid attending parties these days but for different reasons. Neal avoids attending parties because he's anxious when he speaks to people he doesn't know well. Nell avoids attending parties because she's depressed and believes she won't enjoy a party the way she once did, so what's the point.

Neal and Nell both meet with counselors, and their counselors tell them the same thing. In order to feel better, it's necessary for you to face your anxious or depressed feelings, and the easiest way to do that is to face them one step at a time.

for you to do

Facing unpleasant feelings isn't easy. That's why it helps to build a ladder of steps. First, identify your goal. For example, if you avoid enclosed spaces because you feel anxious, your goal might be to feel comfortable in enclosed spaces that are safe, such as elevators. If you avoid doing fun things that were once fun because you're depressed, your goal might be to feel less depressed doing fun things. Next, list as many small *steps* as you can think of and rate each step (from 0 to 10, where 10 is very uncomfortable) relative to how uncomfortable you'll feel if you do the step. Last, order them from lowest level of discomfort to highest level of discomfort. To get an idea of how to do this, look at the ladders that Neal and Nell created.

Neal			Nell		
Goal: Feel less anxious at parties speaking with people I don't know well.			*Goal:* Feel less depressed doing things that once were fun—like parties.		
Step 1:	Smile at people on the street I don't know.	2	*Step 1:*	Watch my favorite funny show with Mom.	3
Step 2:	Order pizza on phone, ask person their name.	4	*Step 2:*	Walk my dog around the park on a sunny day.	5
Step 3:	Ask person who delivers pizza their name.	7	*Step 3:*	Call LaShawn and talk with her for twenty minutes.	7
Step 4:	Compliment a stranger about their clothes.	8	*Step 4:*	Go to movie with two of my closest friends.	8
Step 5:	Introduce myself to a stranger on the bus.	9	*Step 5:*	Hang out with my friends for half a day.	9

Now, you try it. On a blank sheet of paper, write your goal and the steps in the order you'll face your uncomfortable feelings. You can also download a blank copy of My Face Uncomfortable Feelings Worksheet from http://www.newharbinger.com/49197.

My Face Uncomfortable Feelings Worksheet

Instructions: Write your ***goal*** (for example, to feel less anxious when speaking with people). Write as many small ***steps*** as you can think of and order them relative to the level of ***discomfort*** you'll feel (0 to 10, where 10 is extreme discomfort) if you do that step.

Goal:		
		Discomfort Level
Step 1:		
Step 2:		
Step 3:		
Step 4:		
Step 5:		

more to do

Once you've created your uncomfortable feeling ladder, try each step several times. Stepping toward uncomfortable feelings can be difficult, so you may want to practice with someone who can support you. Think of someone with whom you feel safe and comfortable, and ask the person to help you complete each step of the exercise.

Describe what it was like to face rather than to avoid your uncomfortable feelings.

____

____

____

____

Which step of the feelings ladder was the hardest for you to do? Describe how you might break down that step to make it a little easier next time.

____

____

____

____

Describe how long it took for your uncomfortable feelings to change once you faced them (minutes, hours, days) and what that was like for you.

____

____

____

Describe other situations that trigger your uncomfortable feelings.

___

___

___

___

___

Describe the steps of the ladders you could use to face the above uncomfortable feelings.

___

___

___

___

___

34 float to manage panic

for you to know

A panic attack is a sudden rush of fear or terror that includes intense physical sensations (for example, difficulty breathing, rapid heartbeat, dizziness, or sweating). The first panic attack tends to come out of nowhere, and people often think that they're dying or going crazy. People can learn to manage panic attacks by learning to float with the first signs of panic.

It had been a stressful couple of months for Odette. Her father lost his job, and after many months, he finally found one in another town, which meant that Odette started a new high school with new teachers and new kids. Also, her baby sister had been very ill, and the entire family was worried about her. And as if things couldn't get worse, Odette's mother broke her leg in an auto accident, and then much of the day-to-day work at home fell on Odette's shoulders.

Odette was in geography class when the first panic attack hit. In an instant, her heart started to pound, she felt dizzy, nauseated, and her arms and hands tingled. Mr. Piazza quickly walked to Odette to check on her. He then told Odette to breathe slowly and deeply while she counted to ten. In a minute, the feeling started to pass, but Odette was terrified. She didn't understand what was happening and looked at Mr. Piazza, who said, "I think you had a panic attack." He told her that people have panic attacks when they're under a lot of stress for a long time, and that although panic attacks are very scary, they're not dangerous. Odette felt better hearing that.

Although Odette didn't have another panic attack, she did have panicky feelings all day, as if another panic attack might happen at any time. After school, she walked to Mr. Piazza's classroom. He invited her to sit down. Odette then told him about the panicky feelings and how scary they were. Mr. Piazza said, "Remember the lesson on tides and currents last month? Well, a panic attack is like a rip current." He then reminded her that rip currents are shallow, powerful currents that flow away from the shore. They're only dangerous if you try to swim against them. A rip current is much stronger than any swimmer, and if you swim against it, you'll just get tired and sink. Odette listened and then asked, "So what do you do in a rip current?" Mr. Piazza smiled and said, "You float! The current pulls you out, not down. You float on your back, dog paddle, or even swim in a circle until the current weakens. Then you swim parallel to the shore for a few yards and swim in." Mr. Piazza then added, "The same is true for panic attacks. The best way to prevent a panic attack is to float with those panicky feelings rather than swim against the feelings or fight them. If you try to fight the panicky feelings, you're more likely to have a panic attack."

for you to do

You can learn to float to manage panic if you have a plan. A float-to-manage-panic plan has two parts: tools to calm your mind and tools to calm your body. Here's Odette's float-to-manage-panic plan:

Calm Mind Floating Tools
Remind yourself to float with the feelings rather than try to swim against them: These feelings are like a current or wave. They come and go. I'll just float, float.
Remind yourself that anxiety, panic attacks, and panicky feelings aren't dangerous: These panicky feelings aren't dangerous.
Remind yourself that you can handle these feelings: These feelings are uncomfortable, but I can handle them.
Remind yourself that anxiety and panicky feelings will pass with time: These feelings will pass, if I float with them.
Focus on what is happening now rather than what might happen in the future: In this moment, I'm anxious and uncomfortable, but I'm okay.
Calm Body Floating Tools
Breathe slowly and deeply as you count to ten.
As you breathe and count, imagine the word "relax" in your "mind's eye."
When you open your eyes, say to yourself the names of things around you (for example, couch, rug, book, clock).

Now, you try it. Use the My Float to Manage Panic Plan below, write your own float to manage panic plan, or download a blank copy of the from http://www.newharbinger.com/49197.

My Float to Manage Panic Plan

Instructions: In the ***Calm Mind Floating Tools*** section of the plan, write what you'll say to yourself to calm your mind and encourage yourself to float with the panicky feelings. In the ***Calm Body Floating Tools*** section of the plan, write the relaxation and distraction tools you'll use to calm your body as you float with the panicky feelings.

Calm Mind Floating Tools
Remind yourself to float with the feelings rather than try to swim against them:
Remind yourself that anxiety, panic attacks, and panicky feelings aren't dangerous:
Remind yourself that you can handle these feelings:
Remind yourself that anxiety and panicky feelings will pass with time:
Focus on what is happening now rather than what might happen in the future:
Calm Body Floating Tools

more to do

Describe where you were and what you were feeling and thinking the last time you had a panic attack.

____

____

____

____

Write the most intense and scariest body sensations (for example, heart racing, difficulty breathing, sweating) you had during a panic attack.

____

____

____

____

Describe what happened when you tried to fight or swim against the panicky feelings.

____

____

____

____

If you've had several panic attacks, describe the patterns you've noticed (for example, situations that triggered panic attacks; the most intense, scary body sensations; and what you did).

____

____

____

____

Describe how long the panicky feelings lasted when you swam against the feelings and how long they lasted when you floated with them.

____

____

____

____

35 create a wind-down routine

for you to know

When you're anxious and depressed, you tend to have a busy mind, and a busy mind during the day can make it difficult to settle down and sleep at bedtime. A wind-down routine is a powerful way to signal your mind that it's time to relax, unwind, and move toward sleep. Creating a wind-down routine that you practice every night is a simple and easy skill to help you sleep better.

Anyone who has ever met Aiesha will tell you that she's one of a kind. Everything about her is unique: the way she dresses, the kind of music she likes, even the way she dances. As unique as she is, one thing she has in common with many of her friends is that she has trouble settling down at bedtime. She tends to toss and turn, particularly after a day of racing from one thing to another. During biology, the teacher taught Aiesha's class about the brain, sleep, and the importance of a wind-down routine at bedtime to signal the brain to shift into sleep. Aiesha decides to try it and creates a wind-down routine that is uniquely Aiesha.

for you to do

It's important to create a wind-down routine that is simple and personal. Try to include strategies in your wind-down routine that use all your senses (sight, sound, taste, smell, touch) to signal your brain that it's time to shift down for sleep. Here are several wind-down strategies:

Take a warm bath or shower.	Breathe slowly and deeply for ten minutes.
Listen to a guided relaxation recording.	Stretch gently for ten minutes.
Play calming music that you listen to only during your wind-down routine.	Massage your face and hands with a scented lotion that you apply only at bedtime.
Say a mantra to yourself for five minutes (like "silver moon," "cobalt night," "easy sleep").	Curl up in your warm bed and savor the good things that happened that day.
Meditate for ten minutes.	Listen to a relaxing podcast or audiobook.
Write in your journal for ten minutes, reflecting on the good things about the day.	Drink, smell, and hold a cup of herbal tea that you drink only at bedtime.

Look at the list of wind-down strategies. Which strategies would you consider trying every night for two weeks? Which strategies are off the table?

____

____

____

____

____

more to do

Now that you've identified several wind-down strategies that might work for you, it's time to create a personalized wind-down routine. To get started, look at Aiesha's personalized wind-down routine:

Wind-Down Routine	
Step 1.	Place the soft plush wind-down pillow on my bed. Settle into the pillow and pull up the covers so that I'm warm and cozy.
Step 2.	Place the purple scarf over the bedtable light to dim the room light and give the room a soft, cool glow.
Step 3.	Write in my gratitude journal for ten minutes. Describe at least three things that happened during the day for which I'm grateful.
Step 4.	Sip a cup of warm chamomile tea from my special wind-down mug. Breathe in the warm fragrance of the chamomile tea steeping in the mug.
Step 5.	Listen to a wind-down music playlist that includes calming, relaxing songs while I massage my hands with a lotion I use only at bedtime.

Now, build your own wind-down routine. Use the blank My Wind-Down Routine Worksheet below or download a copy from http://www.newharbinger.com/49197.

My Wind-Down Routine Worksheet

Instructions: Write the steps in your wind-down routine worksheet and try the routine for at least a week. Each day, rate how well the wind-down routine helped prepare your mind and body for sleep. Use a 0 to 10 scale (where 10 is a bullseye, 5 is close but not great, and 0 is not helpful at all).

Day of ____________________	
Wind-Down Routine	
Step 1.	
Step 2.	
Step 3.	
Step 4.	
Step 5.	

Look at the wind-down routines that you tried. Which routine did you like the most?

____

____

Which one worked the best?

____

____

Which one worked the least?

____

____

exercise to feel better 36

for you to know

Exercise is a powerful method to reduce anxiety and depression. You'll notice the benefits while you exercise and for hours and days afterward. It's important to include regular exercise in your plan to lessen your anxiety and depression.

When we exercise, magical things happen. We release chemicals in our brains and bodies that neutralize stress chemicals and stimulate the release of "happiness chemicals" called endorphins. These "happiness chemicals" are a powerful antidote to anxiety and depression. In addition to reducing anxiety and depression, there are other benefits to regular exercise:

- **Exercise builds self-confidence and self-esteem.** When you exercise regularly, you'll grow stronger mentally and physically, and therefore more confident that you can handle life's challenges. You'll become stronger and more coordinated and feel better about your appearance. This will increase your social confidence.
- **Exercise sharpens memory and thinking.** The same "happiness chemicals" that make you feel better also help you concentrate and feel mentally sharp. Exercise also stimulates the growth of new brain cells that can help you learn and thrive.
- **Exercise improves sleep.** Even short bursts of exercise in the morning or afternoon can help regulate your sleep patterns. Exercise improves the quality of your sleep because you'll sleep more deeply. If you prefer to exercise at night, relaxing exercises such as yoga or gentle stretching can help promote sleep, so long as you don't exercise too close to bedtime.
- **Exercise increases energy.** Although you expend energy when you exercise, over time, you increase your body's energy reserves. More energy gives you more

get-up-and-go, which counters the fatigue you feel when you're stressed or down. Also, with more energy, you'll get more things off your to-do list, which will lower your stress and improve your mood.

- **Exercise increases resilience**. Exercise improves your ability to bounce back from the physical and emotional challenges you face. As you build an exercise habit, you'll notice that the small tasks that once overwhelmed you now seem more reasonable and doable.

for you to do

To begin your exercise program, start by creating a plan. An effective exercise plan includes the exercise you'll do, the amount you'll do, and when you'll do it.

Circle any of the following types of exercise that sound like fun:

Basketball	Frisbee golf	Rock climbing	Tennis
Biking	Hiking	Running	Volleyball
Calisthenics	Jumping rope	Shadowboxing	Walking
Circuit training	Karate	Skateboarding	Wall ball
Dancing	Power walking	Squash	Weight lifting
Exercise bike	Racquetball	Swimming	Yoga

List any other types of exercise that aren't listed but you've wanted to try.

___

___

___

To make exercise more fun, consider asking a friend to be your exercise buddy. List the friends you'll ask:

___

___

___

Now, decide how often you'll do the exercise. Remember to set a realistic goal that starts where you are. If you haven't exercised in a long time, set a goal of exercising once or twice each week.

___

___

___

What's the best day and time to exercise? Be realistic here too. If you're not a morning person, consider exercising a little later in the day, but not late in the evening. Late exercise might keep you awake when you want to sleep.

___

___

___

Last, decide how much time you'll exercise. Remember to start small, perhaps fifteen minutes at first, and then increase the amount of time you exercise over the next few months.

____

____

____

Now, put these pieces together and create your exercise plan below:

Day	Time	Exercise	Amount
Monday	3:30 p.m.	Jump rope	10 mins.
Wednesday	2:45 p.m.	Dance in my room	15 mins.
Friday	3:30 p.m.	Jumping jacks	10 mins.

more to do

To build an exercise habit, record when you exercise and the amount of exercise you do. Circle the number that corresponds to the level (where 1 is low and 5 is high) of anxiety or depression you feel *before* and *after* you exercise. Use the blank My Exercise to Feel Better Log below or download a blank copy from http://www.newharbinger.com/49197.

My Exercise to Feel Better Log

Instructions: Record the day you exercise and the amount of exercise you do. Then, circle the number that corresponds to the level (where 1 is low and 5 is high) of anxiety or depression you feel ***before*** and ***after*** you exercise.

Week of		Anxiety or Depression									
Day	*Amount*	*Before Exercise*					*After Exercise*				
		1	2	3	4	5	1	2	3	4	5
		1	2	3	4	5	1	2	3	4	5
		1	2	3	4	5	1	2	3	4	5
		1	2	3	4	5	1	2	3	4	5
		1	2	3	4	5	1	2	3	4	5
		1	2	3	4	5	1	2	3	4	5
		1	2	3	4	5	1	2	3	4	5

Review your anxiety or depression ratings for the week. Describe how your anxious or depressed feelings changed from before to after you exercised.

___

___

___

___

___

If you weren't able to accomplish your exercise goal for the week, explain what you think got in the way.

___

___

___

___

___

eat healthy to feel better 37

for you to know

When you're anxious or depressed, you can fall into a pattern of unhealthy eating. You might eat high-calorie foods to boost your mood. You might use caffeinated beverages to boost your energy after a day of the blahs. You might eat fast food because you're too stressed or down to prepare a healthy meal. Developing a plan can help you break these unhealthy eating patterns that inflame your anxiety and depression.

In order to develop a healthy eating plan, it's important to consider the three Ws of healthy eating:

1. **What you eat:** Food fuels a body the way gas fuels a car. When you mainly fill a car's tank with low-grade fuel, you can expect that it will run poorly or even break down. Fill your tank with healthy foods first, then there will be less room for unhealthy foods. Start with colorful fruits and vegetables. Top off the tank, if you wish, with less colorful foods, like those beige and brown chips or cookies. Beware, though—food companies know the trick about color. Start with foods that naturally have color rather than foods that companies add color to, such as those multicolored chips.
2. **When you eat:** When you eat can make a difference. Late-night eating, for example, affects your circadian, or biological, clock. That's the clock that regulates important biological functions such as sleep, hormone secretion, blood pressure, and metabolism. Healthy eating involves eating on a reasonable schedule and avoiding late-night snacks.

3. **Where and how you eat:** Eating on the run or eating while doing something else isn't healthy eating because it's not mindful eating. Mindful eating is when you pay close attention to what you're eating. Mindful eating also makes you less likely to race past the "tank-is-full" warning your stomach sends to your brain when you've eaten enough. In order to eat more mindfully, don't read, text, or watch videos while you eat. If you're eating, just eat. Also, sit down when you eat. Sitting down can help remind you to eat at a slower pace and pay attention to your stomach's signal that the tank is full.

for you to do

Now, use the three Ws to create a healthy eating plan. Record your anxiety and depression each day. Use the blank My Eat Healthy to Feel Better Log below or download a blank copy from http://www.newharbinger.com/49197.

My Eat Healthy to Feel Better Log

Instructions: For each day of the week, record when (time of day) you ate, where and how (e.g., standing at counter texting) you ate, and what (all food and beverages) you ate. Then, circle the number that corresponds to the level (where 1 is low and 5 is high) of anxiety or depression you felt in the ***morning***, ***afternoon***, and ***evening.***

Week of				**Anxiety or Depression**														
Day of Week	*When You Ate*	*Where and How You Ate*	*What You Ate*	*Morning*					*Afternoon*					*Evening*				
Sun				1	2	3	4	5	1	2	3	4	5	1	2	3	4	5
Mon				1	2	3	4	5	1	2	3	4	5	1	2	3	4	5
Tues				1	2	3	4	5	1	2	3	4	5	1	2	3	4	5
Wed				1	2	3	4	5	1	2	3	4	5	1	2	3	4	5
Thurs				1	2	3	4	5	1	2	3	4	5	1	2	3	4	5
Fri				1	2	3	4	5	1	2	3	4	5	1	2	3	4	5
Sat				1	2	3	4	5	1	2	3	4	5	1	2	3	4	5

more to do

Look over the information you recorded about your eating habits. Describe the patterns you notice between when, where, how, and what you eat and your levels of anxiety or depression.

___

___

___

Describe ways you could improve your eating habits. Consider all of the three Ws.

___

___

___

conclusion

Congratulations! You've completed the workbook. In the process of working through the thirty-seven activities, you've learned skills to help you manage your anxiety and depression, as well as the occasional bout of nervousness or blues. As simple as these activities are, they're not fluff. Many decades of research tell us that the skills in these activities work for anxious and depressed teens. With some practice, they'll work for you too. Then the days will feel easier because you'll feel more confident, capable, and ready to take on life!

You may have noticed that certain activities work better for you than others. That's okay. However, if one day you notice that your favorite activities don't seem to be enough, review the workbook and try some of the other ones. A workbook with thirty-seven activities means that you're likely to find one or two more activities that help.

Also, keep in mind that though this workbook is for teens, this doesn't mean that the activities in the workbook won't help when you're older. Any change and any challenge, whether starting college or your first job, can set off your anxiety or depression—and the activities in this workbook that helped you now, in your teen years, can help you when you're older and for many years to come.

Last, if your anxiety or depression persists after practicing the activities in the workbook for several weeks or months, you might want to seek the support of a counselor who can tailor the workbook activities to fit you and your particular circumstances. A bit of additional support may be all you need to turn the corner. However, if your anxiety or depression worsens over time and, in particular, if you're having thoughts of hurting yourself, tell a caring adult who can keep you safe while you find a counselor who can help.

Millions of teens suffer with anxiety, depression, or both, and millions of teens overcome these feelings to live full and successful lives. You, too, can be one of those teens. It just takes a bit of wisdom, practice, and support along the way. Good luck!

Michael A. Tompkins, PhD, ABPP, is a board-certified psychologist in behavioral and cognitive psychology. He is codirector of the San Francisco Bay Area Center for Cognitive Therapy, and is a faculty member of the Beck Institute for Cognitive Behavior Therapy. Tompkins is author or coauthor of fifteen books, and presents to national and international audiences on cognitive behavioral therapy (CBT) and related topics. His work has been highlighted by media outlets, including in *The New York Times, The Wall Street Journal,* on television (The Learning Channel, A&E), and on radio (KQED, NPR).

Did you know there are **free tools** you can download for this book?

Free tools are things like **worksheets**, **guided meditation exercises**, and **more** that will help you get the most out of your book.

You can download free tools for this book—whether you bought or borrowed it, in any format, from any source—from the New Harbinger website. All you need is a NewHarbinger.com account. Just use the URL provided in this book to view the free tools that are available for it. Then, click on the "download" button for the free tool you want, and follow the prompts that appear to log in to your NewHarbinger.com account and download the material.

You can also save the free tools for this book to your **Free Tools Library** so you can access them again anytime, just by logging in to your account! Just look for this button on the book's free tools page.

+ Save this to my free tools library

If you need help accessing or downloading free tools, visit **newharbinger.com/faq** or contact us at **customerservice@newharbinger.com.**